Ghosts Around the House

BOOKS BY SUSY SMITH

The Mediumship of Mrs. Leonard
The Enigma of Out-of-Body Travel
ESP for the Millions
A Supernatural Primer for the Millions
Haunted Houses for the Millions
Out-of-Body Experiences for the Millions
Reincarnation for the Millions
World of the Strange
ESP
Widespread Psychic Wonders
ESP and Sex
Today's Witches
Psychic Animals
Prominent American Ghosts
Ghosts Around the House

GHOSTS
Around the
HOUSE

Susy Smith

THE WORLD PUBLISHING COMPANY

New York and Cleveland

Published by The World Publishing Company
2231 West 110th Street, Cleveland, Ohio 44102
Published simultaneously in Canada by
Nelson, Foster & Scott Ltd.

First Printing—1970

Library of Congress Catalog Card Number: 70–100108

Printed in the United States of America

WORLD PUBLISHING
TIMES MIRROR

Contents

Preface

PUBLISHERS LOVE TO have their authors make appearances on television and radio when a new book comes out; and the communications people appreciate having an author because they usually get some good conversation about a topic of interest. If you have a book to plug, you are happy to be interviewed because it gives you an opportunity to discuss your favorite ideas. When invited to appear, I am delighted to discuss any phase of psychical research because I am so enthusiastic about it. But most of all I am glad to go before the public because I have received so much interesting material from my listeners.

As readers of *Prominent American Ghosts* will recall, it was while I was appearing on Bill Smith's "Talk of Miami" radio program on WKAT that a woman called in and told me about the peculiar activity that was going on at the Tropication Arts warehouse where she worked. Things were falling off shelves when nobody was near, she said. This led me to visit the warehouse and discover the wonderful Miami poltergeist, which is still making history in psychical circles because of its evidence of authenticity.

It was while I was writing this present book, the sequel to *Prominent American Ghosts*, that I was asked to appear on WAJA, Channel 23, a local Miami television station, on Tuesday, January 21, 1969, exactly two years from the time the poltergeist was performing in the warehouse. I was interviewed by Alan Rock on "Talk Back," a program on which listeners called in to ask questions and give comments. This one television program was responsible for my receiving *three* messages that were of assistance in writing this book.

There was a television photographer named David Haylock who had been at the Tropication Arts warehouse during the time of the poltergeist activity. Unfortunately, he left before I could get his testimony, but I knew that he had been impressed with what he had seen there. I did not know how to locate him, but on the "Talk Back" program someone who called mentioned Dave Haylock as having told her about the interesting experience he'd had there. I acquired his telephone number from her, and reached Dave on the phone that weekend. The testimony he gave me was very helpful for the defense, even if a bit late.

David Haylock informed me that he had kept a watchful eye on Julio Vasquez, the boy around whom the poltergeist activity centered, but he had observed nothing in any way incriminating. Dave was photographing the activity in the warehouse for European television. For this reason he took many still pictures and also kept his television camera trained on Julio much of the time. He told me, "I was seriously trying to catch Julio at it, but several things occurred when he was nowhere close enough to the activity to have been able to cause it in any normal way— with his hands or strings or wires or a stick or anything else. Also I was watching him when he did not know it, and I never saw him do anything suspicious. I can state that although I think the activity was somehow associated with Julio, through the power of his mind or in some other inexplicable way, the boy was not doing it by any physical means."

This was the same general conclusion reached by W. G. Roll

of the Psychical Research Foundation of Durham, North Carolina, who came to Miami to investigate the warehouse case. Quite naturally I was delighted to receive further corroboration, for I am still far out in left field with the local newspapers and some others because of my stanch defense of the genuinely supernormal nature of the Miami poltergeist phenomena.

David Haylock expressed himself as willing to show his pictures to Roll or to anyone else who would like to examine them. This present book, of course, will bring everyone up to date on what has happened to Julio since he left the warehouse—including the testimony of several new employers whose dishes dashed and bottles crashed while he was there.

Later on the "Talk Back" program Vangie White called me to say "hello." She did not know she was lost; but I had been trying for months to locate her to obtain permission to use her name and her story here. Now, with her blessing, "The C. Harvey W. Caper" is ready to read. Vangie had acquired a divorce, a new husband and a new name since I saw her last, so it is not surprising that she had disappeared from her old neighborhood.

The third event of interest involving my television appearance on January 21 came from June Witlin of Miami Beach, a lady who is unknown to me except for her call. She had never seen me before, either, until she happened to tune in that night. She was not able to get a studio line until the program was over, and it was then that she told me she had called to inform me that I had a ghost.

Now seeing ghosts on your television screen is not unusual for anyone whose set is not correctly adjusted. But in the picture on her tube Mrs. Witlin saw a real, live ghost standing behind my chair, right back of my left shoulder. It was apparently some relative of mine who was sharing the pleasure of the interview with me—invisible to all except June Witlin.

I was interested, and asked for a description of my unusual visitor. Mrs. Witlin began by saying that she thought it probably was my grandmother because she looked to be about sixty to sixty-five years old. She was tall and a rather large woman, although not fat. "You resemble her," my caller said. This description sounded somewhat like my mother to me, so I encouraged Mrs. Witlin to continue, without telling her who I thought it was. She said the ghost had a pleasant face, looking as if she were very goodnatured and full of fun. My mother exactly. She said she wore a simple dress—Mother would never wear anything the least elaborate. Finally I said, "Mrs. Witlin, is this my grandmother, are you sure?" She replied, "Either that or your mother. I thought because she looked about sixty or a little older that she must be your grandmother." I was flattered but admitted that my mother had died at sixty, and that this description fitted her very well.

Toward the end of our conversation Mrs. Witlin added the icing to the cake. She described my ghostly visitor's hair: "It was graying, and sort of pulled back at the sides with a large wave." That cinched it. The one and only thing Mother had the least vanity about was her hair, a gorgeous auburn until it began to gray. Combing that wave carefully was the only primping she ever did.

No picture of my mother has ever been published. Mrs. Witlin and I are not acquainted, and she has certainly never been in my home where she could have seen a photograph of my mother. Neither do I think her description fits "just anyone." She hit exactly with every point she mentioned: the height and size, the coloring, the likeness between us, the expression and character, the age, and then to top it off—the wave.

I must say, to have my deceased mother seen on a television program with me was very heartwarming. How is it, though, that just one person can see a ghost when others do not? I heard from no one else who had observed her. This is one of the big questions about ghosts. It is also one of the main points in the arguments of those who insist all ghosts are hallucinations. On occasion a roomful of persons has had a ghost in the midst of it and everyone present has seen it except one individual. That prosaic

man has stoutly maintained that everyone else is out of his cot-
ton-pickin' mind and claiming to see things that do not exist. One
can hardly blame him. And yet if this same individual were to
happen to be the only person in the room to see a phantom when
it was invisible to the rest, he would have quite a different story
to tell. Historically, such things may happen either way, although
why I do not know.

There is no doubt about it, ghosts are arbitrary, difficult, confusing, and befuddling. They are also very interesting. It would
seem to be wise here to discuss the various types of spectral manifestations for the reader who comes to this for the first time,
even though it may be somewhat repetitive to ardent phantom
fanciers.

There are at least four different kinds of ghosts—possibly more,
when we learn more about them. One type gives evidence of
being a deceased human being now surviving in the spirit world
who wishes to make himself seen for the purpose of bringing information: serving notice of his death, telling where a lost will
can be found, or, as in the case of Loretta Butcher's father, keeping a promise.

Mrs. Butcher moved to Logan, West Virginia, when she married, while her parents remained at their home near Washington,
D.C. Her father, Charles Prince, often promised to visit her but
something always delayed him.

Loretta says in *Fate* magazine, March 1969, that she had not
been home in nine years when, on June 12, 1958, her mother
wrote that her father had been operated on for cancer but was
now doing fine. "Her cheerful tone was reassuring," Mrs. Butcher
says.

Early on the morning of June 21, 1958, a knock on the front
door awakened her. A thunderstorm was raging outside, and she
returned to sleep. Then the knock came again, this time on her
bedroom door.

Loretta Butcher says, "Thinking one of my children might be
scared or sick I got up and slipped on a robe. When I opened

my bedroom door, there stood Dad, clearly visible in the dim light we kept burning in the hall. He was very pale and looked very tired."

"Why Dad," she beamed, "what a surprise! Why didn't you let me know you were coming!"

He smiled at her and said, "I have kept my promise." Then, Mrs. Butcher says, "I threw my arms around his neck only to clutch thin air. He had turned to mist."

Mrs. Butcher's bedside clock read 4:00 A.M., but there was no more sleep for her that night. At 7:15 her mother telephoned to tell her that her father had died at four o'clock. He *had* kept his promise to visit her.

There is another kind of ghost that is hallucination, pure and simple. Even whistling when one is walking through a graveyard at night cannot keep the ghosts away if you are apprehensive enough. Any bush may be a spook reaching out to grab you, any fog a full-fleshed apparition. It is even possible, I understand, for one to become so absolutely frantic with fright that he can produce a genuinely materialized ghost by the power of his own thoughts.

Persons who are having out-of-body experiences are on occasion seen by others. This is usually referred to as "bilocation," the idea being that it is possible to be in two places at once. There is enough evidence for this that it must be accepted, although it is difficult to understand. There are those whose conscious minds can actually leave their bodies in such a way that it cannot be confused with daydreaming or any other form of wishful thinking. The consciousness looks down and sees the body lying rigid on the bed, and then it proceeds to move away. It may go only a few feet or it may go miles. Individuals have been seen some distance from home and even conversed with while their physical bodies were asleep in bed. This entity which is seen, the consciousness in some kind of a spirit or astral body, is considered to be a ghost of the living.

Ambrose Worrall of Baltimore and his wife, Olga, are world-famous healers. Once Ambrose dreamed himself into being an out-of-body ghost who was seen by his wife. He was away on business and Olga decided to keep a light burning in the bathroom all night because there had been burglary scares in the neighborhood. This was too much for her husband's Scots blood, even though he was in another town. He came home in his sleep and saw the light on and tried to tell Olga about it. She woke up to see Ambrose looking down at her, his face almost touching hers, and he was impressing her with the thought, "Put out the light! Put out the light!"

Olga Worrall called out, "I see you, darling. What do you want to tell me?" Then he disappeared from view. His wife decided to humor him and got up and doused the lights.

When Ambrose returned home several days later he told his wife that a strange thing had occurred the first night he was away. He had seemed to be dreaming, but later it was reality, for he visited her and talked to her. He had walked through the house and when he passed the bathroom had wondered, "Now why is she wasting money leaving the light on?"

Ambrose told Olga, "With this thought in mind I promptly headed into the bathroom to put out the light. As I touched the switch my hand went right through the wall; it had no effect on the button. Startled, I went into the bedroom and began to call your name. I kept sending the thought, 'Put out the light! Put out out the light!' I heard you say, 'I see you, darling,' and then I found myself back in the hotel bed."

A fourth kind of ghost is what is called a "veridical after-image." The power of the thought of those undergoing some terribly traumatic or dramatic disaster can apparently be so intense that it somehow makes an imprint on the atmosphere. We do not know how this is done. There is much about our world that we do not yet know. Since the splitting of the atom most people will agree to that. We do know, however, that when conditions are right, certain scenes of past events, usually great crimes or battles or massacres, seem to be repeating themselves frequently.

If psychic persons are present, they can see these scenes. Many people who are not critical about psychical phenomena believe that the actual spirits of the individuals continue to go over and over the same scene because they are unable to force themselves to leave it. This reliving of the tragic moment is said to account for the ghostly manifestations that are occasionally reported in haunted houses. I think the veridical after-image is a much better explanation, and one that we will very likely find some means of confirming scientifically in the near future.

As has been seen, not all ghosts are the manifestion of a still-living entity. There are just enough who appear genuinely to be that, however, to titillate our fancy and arouse our desire to learn just how they accomplish their feat of being seen.

It will be noted in this book that a ghost may occasionally just happen to be visible for a few minutes. He may be sighted by anyone as he is passing by, and may disappear as abruptly as he appeared, having been only momentarily perceptible in our realm. What the conditions were that permitted this and why they were right for him to have been seen at all, however briefly, is something for which we have no real explanation.

Of course, there are many strongly psychic people who say they are able to see spirits almost any time. Sometimes they can give so much evidence that we have to accept their stories. When such an individual goes to a haunted house, he may meet all kinds of eerie creatures from the spirit world. When he stays at home, he may commune with his deceased relatives from time to time as a matter of course. Such psychic persons as June Witlin see ghosts so often that they take them in stride and do not get excited about them—unless they happen to view one on television.

In 1966–67 I traveled all over the United States collecting well-known ghost stories in preparation for *Prominent American Ghosts*. After the success of that book, World Publishing Company asked me to do something similar for its sequel *Ghosts Around the House*. During the past year I have again traveled widely, had some interesting experiences, made some new friends, and collected more instances of notable ghosts and famous haunted houses. I have also dug out some of the more obscure cases, which proved to be just as fascinating.

This book does not attempt to give scientific reports or documented evidence of the apparitions it discusses. I leave that to the parapsychologists. Still, there is no fiction here. The subject is treated altogether factually, my main goal being to present genuine and realistic material entertainingly. If the book also indicates that haunting phenomena do appear actually and frequently in the homes of intelligent and critical people, that is a fact of life, so why deny it? We have for too long hidden haunts under a bushel of lies and subterfuge. I think we have been afraid to face the possibility that a certain type of ghost may reveal to us evidence for something that as materialists we have been unwilling to accept—the possibility of life after death.

Now that materialism is no longer in style and we are once again openly seeking the answers to life's primary questions, perhaps a good ghost in the closet from time to time may bring us a message we want to hear.

Ghosts Around the House

CHAPTER I

The Lost Dauphin

THE SOUTHERNMOST POINT of the United States is Key West, Florida, where the Atlantic Ocean meets and mingles with the Gulf of Mexico. There, at a beautiful old home on that farthest reach of land, a friend of mine saw a ghost.

Harry Emerson of Miami was standing on the wide veranda of the dignified mansion built by John H. Geiger. It is now known as the Audubon House because the brilliant naturalist and bird painter once lived there for a time. When Harry saw this elegant, if decidedly ephemeral, dandy dressed in nineteenth-century clothing leaning against the railing opposite him on the porch, he wondered who it could be. He had never heard of Geiger or anyone else associated with the house except Audubon, but he certainly could not dream that this well-dressed phantom was the woodsman, hunter, and painter. As he puzzled over the identification of the ghost, he had the opportunity for a long and careful look at it before it faded away.

Harry told me, "He wore well-tailored clothing—slim trousers, long jacket, and a shirt with a lacy ruffled front. I got a good look at his face, enough that it left a lasting impression. I particularly noticed his height—he was able to brace his backside against the top of the railing, which I with my five foot seven inches could not do."

It was bright daylight, and Emerson has communed with spirits frequently before, so he was not in the least alarmed. He had driven to Key West that pleasant day in the month of July 1968 with an engineer friend who had to repair the recording equipment in the Audubon House. He had several hours to wander around and amuse himself in the captivating old home and its inviting informal gardens. After his ghostly visitor had faded back into the shiplap, Harry went inside, intent upon discovering its identity.

Upstairs there are memorabilia of the great John James Audubon, including several of the bird pictures he painted while staying there. Harry read that the birdman's hour of rising had been three o'clock in the morning; from that time until noon and sometimes even until night, he hunted among the mangrove keys, despite heat, sand-flies, and mosquitoes. On his return from these expeditions he spent all the rest of his waking hours making sketches of the birds and plants he had procured. Indeed, Key West's Audubon House has a rare complete original Double Elephant Folio of his *Birds of America,* those first engravings of his original sketches that were produced between 1826 and 1838.

"There are also," Harry said, "some rather inferior photographs of portraits of Audubon painted by his contemporaries." (Harry Emerson was a photographer for thirty years before his recent retirement, so we should forgive him his professional snobbery.) "There was a great similarity between this face and the one I saw," he said. "But the man in the pictures was dressed as a woodsman; and there was no way to know whether or not he was tall." What Harry then had to learn was if his ghost had represented itself to him accurately. He asked Lillian Stone, the curator of the historical showplace, to tell him more about Audubon—what was he really like? The debonair gentleman was quickly identified by Mrs. Stone. Audubon dressed exquisitely whenever he was not out in the woods bird-hunting, she said. (Indeed, books I have read since that time about Audubon reveal that no matter how elaborately he was gotten up, whether for a dance or party, if he heard the call of a strange bird he was just as likely as not to prance off into the woods and remain for hours, completely oblivious to time, place, or dress.)

When it was suggested that Audubon's ghost had appeared there, Mrs. Stone denied it firmly. She does not believe in such foolishness. She is a very matter-of-fact, no-nonsense woman. She told me when I visited the house with Harry on a later occasion that there was nothing to all that twaddle about Audubon's being the lost Dauphin, either. She was very firm about it.

Harry Emerson is not given to hallucinations, and besides, his ghost brought information about itself that Harry was positive he had not known. But if it really was Audubon's ghost, why was it there? Why return to this house where he had spent, at the most, no more than a few months of his life?

Might we suggest without undue caprice that he came for the purpose of acquiring a place in this book? Perhaps he has left something undone and hopes to arouse further interest in his cause by being written up once again. This baffling pioneer naturalist and artist of distinction may have something more to accomplish before achieving eternal rest. Could he anticipate that his true identity may yet be revealed? Perhaps he wants further research and hopes that we here may be able to arouse enough interest in the question that someone will decide to undertake the job of settling it once and for all. Was he or was he not the lost Dauphin, son of King Louis XVI and Queen Marie Antoinette of France? I must say there seems to be plenty of circumstantial evidence for it, although there is none that is completely convincing.

That Audubon was a man with a lost identity and a great secret there is no doubt. Apparently during his lifetime he was resolved never to reveal the truth. But there is no reason to go down through history as a bastard, either. One can understand that hindsight in the hereafter might have decided him to make further efforts on his own behalf.

His descendants have tried to clear his name, although unsuccessfully. His five granddaughters longed to die in peace, and to keep their big secret from the world. They may have feared that its revelation would force the men in their family to become embroiled in the partisan politics of a friendly nation. All in all, their privacy meant more to them than the prospect of belated prestige. So the Audubon ladies entrusted to the son of one of the five, Leonard Sanford Tyler, and his wife, Alice Jaynes Tyler, their evidence for the truth of their great family secret, with the provision that publication would be withheld until after their own deaths.

The granddaughters reckoned without biographer Francis H. Herrick, who industriously dug out what he considered to be evidence that Audubon was illegitimate, and published it in *Audubon the Naturalist*. This was just too much. The Audubon ladies decided after all to reveal their own suspicions about their grandfather's origin—which were quite different. They gave permission to Alice Jaynes Tyler to publish their grounds for belief that Audubon was the lost Dauphin. Unfortunately, they apparently had no genuine evidence to back up their statements because of their previous meddling with their grandfather's effects. In *I Who Should Command All*, published in 1937, Mrs. Tyler reveals the secret, but also discloses that Maria Audubon, one of the five, had picked and chosen among the naturalist's letters and journals and evidently lost for posterity the originals of the material she felt to be of value. Mrs. Tyler says that both branches of the family had given Maria full authority to use her sole discretion in selecting for publication those portions of John James Audubon's papers which she considered it wise to preserve, and to eliminate those she deemed it expedient to conceal.

Alice Jaynes Tyler inherited Maria's little black book into which she had copied certain transcripts in her monumental compilation of her grandfather's journals. The passages which in

Maria's opinion threw light on Audubon's identity are verified as authentic by the legal affidavit of Harriet Audubon that these quotations were portions of letters written by her grandfather that she had read. But no matter how much verification there is of the copies, the originals would bear considerably more weight.

Harriet had been raised by her grandmother Lucy Bakewell Audubon, that wonderful wife and helpmate who had stood behind the naturalist throughout all his days and survived him by some twenty-three years. After Audubon's death Lucy and Harriet lived for a time at the Manhattanville home of the Reverend Charles Coffin Adams. Mr. Adams was preparing the first Audubon biography, which purported to be the work of his widow.

As Mrs. Tyler tells the story, one day Harriet was sitting at her grandmother's knee while Mr. Adams was working on the Audubon papers in an adjoining room. Suddenly he rushed into their presence, greatly elated, and waved some papers before Lucy. Excitedly he exclaimed, "Madame Audubon, Madame Audubon! I have found out who your husband was! He was the Dauphin!"

Harriet had spent her childhood among those grandchildren whose curiosity as to who Audubon really was had never been appeased. So she watched her grandmother intently. At last she was to find out the truth. She waited breathlessly to see what Lucy would say or do. Lucy turned white as a sheet, and then she flushed all over her face and neck. She did not speak, neither to admit nor to deny it. She just sat silent. She could not speak without breaking her pledge to her husband; and she would not lie to deny it. And so she sat, in perfect silence. The Reverend Mr. Adams understood and wordlessly left the room.

All of the young Audubon ladies were gathered around when, upon the death of Lucy Bakewell Audubon's son Victor, the bereaved mother rushed to his side. Throwing herself on his corpse, Madame Lucy sobbed, so that all the girls could hear, "Oh, my son! My son! And to think I never told you who you are!"

With that sort of thing going on from time to time in your family, it would be difficult not to think there was something very special about this grandfather with the big secret.

In his evaluation of the naturalist and his work titled *John James Audubon,* Dr. Robert Cushman Murphy of the American Museum of Natural History says that to make Audubon good copy the legends of his career unite with the facts in the many books that have appeared about him, "for there is much that still remains clouded with uncertainty or mystery. Even the place, date, and circumstances of his birth are perhaps not settled with finality." But the best source of material about him is his own records "such as drawings, letters, and journals (particularly such as have not been transcribed, smoothed, or emasculated by some of his descendants). . . ." Naturally, a scientist is not going to admit himself to be convinced by all that falderol about Audubon being the lost Dauphin! But he can hint, can't he?

Anyone had only to look at John James Audubon to know he was something very special; and to know him was to be constantly amazed at his talent, charm, versatility, and ability in almost every line. He was indeed a superior specimen of mankind. Dr. Murphy says, "It would be hard to find another historical figure of the 19th century in which superlative traits, both physical and mental, seem to have been more inextricably mingled." He adds that Audubon was beyond any doubt a highly gifted human being. Some of his casually recorded but well-attested accomplishments demonstrate this. Physically he was not only handsome and well formed, but also agile, graceful, wiry, and tireless. He had strength, keenness of sense, poise, and unusual muscular coordination. He danced so well that he was a favorite teacher of the young ladies wherever he went. He could ride any horse and swim any torrent. He could walk with gun and pack from sunrise to sunset, and had been known to travel on foot at the rate of thirty-seven miles a day. He was also an expert fencer and fencing teacher.

In the woods Audubon never got lost. He had a way with Indians as if he had been raised among them. And, to use Murphy's phrases, "He was also a Dead-eye-Dick with the flintlock, and with the percussion fowling pieces used by sportsmen in his latter days." He skated exceptionally well—a graceful and energetic figure gliding over the ice, his white lace fluttering at throat and wrists. For yes, except for the times when he was dressed for traipsing in the woods he always wore fashionable attire and gave every evidence of being a pampered son of indulgent parents of means. He could play the violin, flute, and flageolet well enough to make his living teaching music when it was necessary. And not only could he draw and paint, he could do so with either hand, or with both hands together and simultaneously. "He also," says Dr. Murphy, "possessed the ability to express his thoughts strikingly and picturesquely in three languages, French, Spanish, and English, none of which, according to his own testimony, he spoke with scholarly precision." If his syntax and spelling were outlandish—who cares, with all those other things going for him?

We must not forget to mention the fact that Audubon had exemplary personal habits as well: he rarely drank liquor, tea, or coffee, nor used tobacco. And he eschewed amorous adventures. He lost his heart but once in all his life—to Lucy Bakewell. He was devoted to her from the moment he first met her until death.

It is only fair to admit that he had a few faults as well. Too much perfection could have made him dull. So we learn from the records that in his youth he was filled with a vanity little short of childish. He was also quick-tempered, inordinately moody, and at times vituperative.

Now that we have the character and attributes of this highly unusual man, let us briefly summarize his life from the data known about him. We will go into the suppositions and suspicions later. The facts alone are a colorful story.

There was once a Frenchman named Jean Audubon, the son of Capt. Pierre Audubon, who sailed the seas with considerable success. In 1772 Jean, in France, married a rich widow, Anne Moynette, nine years his senior. Anne remained thereafter at home in Nantes while Jean returned to the sea, and to the ladies who lived in foreign ports. As an admiral, he joined the American Revolutionary forces against the English, commanding a corvette; and he participated in the defeat of Cornwallis at Yorktown. In America Jean Audubon became friends with Gen. George Washington and, with his fellow Frenchman Lafayette, he was converted to the principles of democracy. Yet when he made out his will he signed at the bottom of it "Vive le Roi." So you could say he was a man of many parts and varied convictions.

While living in Santo Domingo Audubon received a carefully itemized bill from a Dr. Sanson revealing that on April 26, 1785, at Aux Cayes, a baby boy was delivered to a Mlle Rabin, a Creole. This child's name was not given, but he was presumed to be Jean Audubon's natural son. It was his discovery of this bill that led Francis Herrick to become convinced that John James Audubon was this illegitimate child.

On March 7, 1794, a nine-year-old boy and a girl named Rosa were legally adopted by Jean Audubon in Nantes. The name of the mother of the girl is carefully given, Catherine Bouffard. The name of the mother of the boy is carefully not given, although, had the boy been the one born in Santo Domingo, her name was known. Mrs. Tyler thinks this significant. She asks, "Does it appear plausible that Jean Audubon, a sound businessman, accustomed to drawing legal documents, should suddenly lapse into laxness and inaccuracy?"

The date of this adoption was just a few months after the Dauphin, a little boy of this same age, had allegedly been spirited out of the Temple in which he had been jailed. But we will go into his story later. For now we are supposed to wonder why Jean Audubon chose this specific time to adopt a boy if it were the same boy who had been born in Santo Domingo, and if this boy had been living with him for nine years without any previous intimation of the need for legal adoption.

Among other curious features of John James Audubon's childhood is that he himself reported in his journal that he had always been carefully attended by two black servants; and that Anne Moynette Audubon had determined he should be brought up a gentleman and had always overindulged him. This is a nice but very singular way to treat one's husband's illegitimate offspring.

Of the years of John James Audubon's life between 1796 and 1800 there are no records. Alice Jaynes Tyler believes from some of his comments in letters to his wife that he was taken to the Earl of Selkirk's settlement in the Hudson Bay region of Canada. This would account, as no upbringing in France possibly could, for his transformation into a powerful, resourceful woodsman. His background indicated that he had been reared in comparative luxury. He dressed with meticulous care, indulging in the finest of linens and fabrics. His tastes were those of one accustomed to wealth. And yet, when John James Audubon came to the United States in 1803, at barely eighteen years of age, he could traverse the continent alone like an Indian, find his way through trackless forests, swim swollen rivers, shoot with the marksmanship of the wilderness, and he could survive with his naked fists in the primeval forests of North America. His contacts with the Indians had the sure touch of easy familiarity; his knowledge of wildlife knew no bounds.

Where had John Audubon acquired this forest training?

Mrs. Tyler says: "It is my belief that he acquired all his forest training in the Selkirk's Settlements, somewhere between 1796 and 1800."

After 1800 the fifteen-year-old boy was back in Nantes again, being sent to the best schools, and attended with Jean and Anne Audubon's exaggerated solicitude. Since he insisted that tracking and painting birds was to be his life's work, he was sent to Paris to study under David, the leading artist of that day.

When John James was eighteen he migrated to America to manage Mill Grove, Jean Audubon's Pennsylvania estate fifteen miles northwest of Philadelphia. Nearby was the home of lovely, gently reared Lucy Bakewell—and from the time he met her he never paid serious attention to any other woman for the rest of his life. On April 8, 1808, they were married and set out immediately by stage and riverboat on a grueling trip to Louisville, Kentucky. Then followed years of hard times and hard work as John James Audubon tried to make a living by orthodox means while his heart was always away in the wild woods with his birds. His physical presence just as often accompanied his heart into the brush while business was left undone.

John and a partner unsuccessfully conducted a store in Louisville and later a lumber and grist mill at Henderson, Kentucky. The partner complained because Audubon neglected business for bird watching; and John admitted it. In an introductory statement he later wrote for one of his books he said, "For a period of nearly twenty years, my life was a succession of vicissitudes. I tried various branches of commerce, but they all proved unprofitable, doubtless because my whole mind was ever filled with my passion for rambling and admiring those objects of nature from which alone I received the purest gratification."

Yet during this time Audubon made beautiful drawings of all the different birds that fell before his gun, and he began a collection of notes on their habits and habitats that was eventually to become one of the first ornithological records in America.

His wife, Lucy, and their two sons, Victor Gifford Audubon and John Woodhouse Audubon, shared with John James his belief in the value of his paintings; and finally Lucy convinced him that he should give up business and dedicate his entire life to his birds. To have a working wife is looked on as an asset in these days; in Audubon's time it was a pure embarrassment. Nonetheless, John and Lucy were both up to the social inconveniences it caused them; and when his efforts won him fame all the people who had talked about them changed their tune quickly.

Lucy lived with a wealthy Louisiana family on their plantation and taught their children in order to make money for herself and the boys; and Audubon took his bird pictures to New

York and Philadelphia, seeking a publisher for his work. Returning, unsuccessful, to Louisiana, he decided that he should try to get help in England. After more effort on the part of both John and Lucy and much saving, eventually he had enough money to make the trip. In May 1826 he sailed from New Orleans for Liverpool.

During the next thirteen years Audubon spent much of his time in England and Scotland. His work was appreciated abroad as it had never been at home, and he eventually secured advance subscriptions to pay for the publication of the gigantic book he envisioned. It was difficult, however, to find someone who could prepare the engravings that were to reproduce the life-size drawings of the American birds exactly as he had made them. Slowly and painstakingly the plates were finished, and *Birds of America* began to appear in installments. The last of the work was published in London in 1838. The books, so very large, are known as Elephant Folio size.

After the publication of these books, only a few of which are now extant in their complete form, Audubon's fame was assured. From then on he was a much-fêted celebrity. On one of his return trips to America he made journeys studying the birdlife at various points along the Atlantic Coast, as far north as Labrador and as far south as Key West—where he lived in the house where his ghost was seen by Harry Emerson.

By 1842 Audubon and his family were established in a new home overlooking the Hudson River just above New York City. In the surrounding grove, houses were built for his two sons and their families. Audubon died January 27, 1851, in his sixty-sixth year, at the height of his renown. Lucy lived until June 13, 1874, and she continued to teach children on and off until her death. She could not change her lifelong habits any more than her husband could have altered his.

Now, what is all this about John James Audubon being the lost Dauphin? First we have to establish that the Dauphin was actually lost. There has been controversy about that, too.

There are so many papers about the French Revolution in so many archives that anyone who undertakes to do research among them has a wealth of data at his disposal, almost too much of it to endure plowing through. Several authors have researched the material, however, for details about the jailing of the King and Queen and their children; and G. LeNotre's work entitled *The Dauphin* (*Louis XVII*), *The Riddle of the Temple* gives us much substantial information to consider, based entirely on official documents and authorized testimony. According to this account of the Dauphin's imprisonment, the story goes as follows:

Louis Charles, the Duc de Normandie, was born March 27, 1785, to Marie Antoinette and Louis XVI of France. There was some gossip at that time of his having had some other father than Louis, but that all blew over. His older brother died four years later and Charles became the Dauphin, the next in succession to the throne. On July 14, 1789, the Bastille fell and the French Revolution went into full swing. Mobs stormed Versailles (the King's country palace) and the royal family moved into the Tuileries in Paris, where they found themselves to be virtual prisoners. On August 13 of the year laughing little prince Charles, whom the French nation loved, was six years old, the royal family was taken prisoner and placed in the Tower of the Temple, a large fortresslike building. In addition to the King and Queen, the party of prisoners consisted of Louis XVI's sister, Mme Elizabeth, and the Dauphin, and his older sister Marie Thérèse, known as Mme Royal. The King and Queen made every effort to keep their family life as nearly normal as possible while in prison, and they played and read with their children, concentrating on their education.

After Louis XVI was taken from them and assassinated, Charles was told by his mother that he was now King Louis XVII. He was old enough to realize the responsibility of this title, although he never had the opportunity to wear it publicly. The boy at this time was most precocious, with a very alert mind; and those exercise books of his which have been preserved show great application and constant progress. LeNotre says, "The little Dauphin found grace in the eyes of the most arrogant." He describes Charles's prettiness, vivacity and intelligence, his animation when at play, his love for his mother, and his frolicsome gaiety which filled the whole prison with joy. This engaging child charmed the most unbending of the municipal officers and one of them confessed that he could not resist the temptation of drawing him aside to embrace him. His especial fondness for birds is noteworthy in the light of our Audubon exploration, for he always insisted upon having as many feathered companions as possible.

LeNotre tells us that in the years of great anguish that followed the death of Louis XVI, when France, disorganized and led astray from the path of its ancient tradition, foresaw the final collapse as imminent, there was to be found, among those who were responsible for the great confusion, a number of sincere patriots who, repenting, made an effort to stem the torrent. Even then there was some plotting for the escape of the Dauphin. But the time was not yet.

The Queen was taken to the guillotine and her children were separated, never to meet again. Mme Royal and Mme Elizabeth remained on the upper floor of the Temple, the boy being kept alone on the ground floor. His sister and aunt could watch the Dauphin, now eight years old, out the window as he ran and played in the courtyard.

The prince's jailers at this time became a man named Simon, a former bootmaker, and his wife, who soon grew fond of their charge. LeNotre says that as a further diversion for his pupil, who had a great desire to keep birds, the shoemaker had an oak aviary with twenty-two perches placed in the embrasure of one of the deep windows of his apartment. Simon was also able to locate for the boy an antique bird cage that was made "entirely of silver with moulded gilded garlands and crystals. It included chimes and a bird organ to instruct the birds. Its construction was admirable, for there were an infinity of drums,

springs, fusées, bellows and triggers, by means of which the
birds, on alighting on one of the perches to eat, made the bird-
organ play."

The authority under whom the Simons held office as the
Dauphin's jailers was Chaumette, who frequently came to visit
the boy. On January 19, 1794, a year after they came to the
Temple, the Simons ostensibly were fired. They gathered all their
property and moved out with a flourish. Mme Simon packed
huge bundles of linen and personally placed them in her push-
cart brought up to the prison door for this purpose. She did not
hesitate to shove aside the prison police when they tried to
examine her bundles—as if she knew she had the authority to
do so. And away she loped into the night, pushing her cart before her.

From this time on, where was that nine-year-old boy who had
been "so engaging through his misfortune and gracefulness, so
full of life, who laughed at every excuse and sang the whole day
long like the birds in his aviary"? He was gone. He was never
seen again. The whole picture of existence at the Temple was
suddenly and inexplicably altered. No doctor ever called after
that; no medications were ever purchased. Chaumette no longer
came to visit his little prisoner. In fact, Chaumette was very soon
afterward imprisoned for plotting to restore the monarchy and
to seat the Dauphin on the throne. Then he was put to death.

Mme Royal, the young princess, wrote in her diary: "On January 19th we heard a great noise at my brother's, which made
us conjecture that he was leaving the Temple, and we were convinced of it, when, looking through a hole in our sun-blind, we
saw many packages being taken away. On the following day
we heard his door open and, still convinced that he was gone,
we believed they had put below some German or foreign prisoner." The princess and her aunt never looked out their window
again to watch a child play in the garden. No child played in
the garden. Apparently the poor little fellow who replaced
Charles was kept shut up all the time so he would not be seen.
No wonder he died within six months.

It was not yet general public knowledge that the Dauphin had escaped. Apparently Robespierre did not even know about it. One night he had the boy removed from the Temple and brought to him for an interview; but he hastily returned him the following night, convinced that he was not the real Dauphin.

His follower, Barras, instituted a new humane regime because of the ever-growing condemnation from the public about the inhumanity of keeping the two innocent children apart in the Temple. He ordered that the Dauphin and his sister, who was now alone since Robespierre had sent Mme Elizabeth to the guillotine, should meet and play together and join each other in the gardens. Mme Royal never once asked to play with the other prisoner, however. She remained convinced that her brother was gone.

The new jailer was M. Laurent, a Creole from Martinique, near Jean Audubon's former rendezvous, Santo Domingo. His appointment indicated an entirely different political policy, and he had the power to do strange things. When Simon, the ex-jailer, was guillotined M. Laurent instantaneously, and on his own initiative, ordered all Simon's papers and effects sealed. This meant that no investigator could get at anything incriminating.

Another questionable point is that when the French government wanted a perfect whitewash and was trying to establish proof beyond doubt that the child who died in the Temple was the real Dauphin, they collected the most bizarre assortment of witnesses to identify him. Citizens came in and declared themselves able to swear to his identity because they had once seen the Dauphin playing in the park, or on the basis of similar inconsequential evidence. All this while Charles's sister was in the room above and could easily have told them if it had really been her brother. Also, Tilson, a former servant of the royal family, was still jailed somewhere in the Temple; but he was never asked to look at the corpse.

Public sentiment took note of the curious conditions surrounding the death. It became widely gossiped about that the Dauphin had escaped and another child had died in his place in the

prison. In fact, before her death, Mme Simon confessed to the
details of how she had spirited the boy out of the Temple in
one of her bundles. During the next few decades there were
some thirty pretenders to the throne who appeared at one place
or another. None of them knew certain essential facts that could
prove them genuine, and so short shrift was made of them. The
most blatant of the pretenders was discovered within weeks of
the January 19 escape. A man made an unnecessarily conspicu-
ous journey over the most traveled highways of France with a
sickly little boy who openly posed as the Dauphin. Most likely
they served as decoys during the time that the real prince was
being spirited away to safety. And, oddly enough, they turned
out to be related to M. Laurent, the Creole, who was now the
jail guard.

Forty-seven days after the January 19 escape, Jean Audubon,
who lived in the south of France, legally adopted a nine-year-
old boy. LaVendee, his home near Nantes, was known as a roy-
alist stronghold, and fighting went on there after all the other
provinces and districts of France became pacified. In LaVendee
now the royalists were aflame with what Alice Jaynes Tyler
refers to as a "passion which seems to have connoted undying
devotion to a personality, for only a personality gives birth to
this type of emotion. Abstract principles cannot evoke it."

Indeed, the leader of the royalists in this area, Gen. Charette,
openly admonished his army in June 1895, "Are you going to let
perish the child so miraculously rescued from the Temple?" But
poor Charette was the one to perish instead. Captured by the
revolutionists, he was put to death. And John James Audubon
was there. Reminiscing in his journal about the incident, he
stated, "I saw him shot on the Place di Viarme at Nantes."

After the death of the protector Charette, nothing more is
heard of "the child so miraculously rescued from the Temple."
Obviously he was taken to some safe place, and probably protected by being made to take oaths never to reveal his secret.

This boy of identical age as the Dauphin, John James Audubon who saw Charette shot at Nantes, suddenly disappears from historical records at just this time, with only oblique references to Selkirk in his later letters to indicate that he might have spent the next four years in that remote settlement in the Hudson Bay country of Canada. These letters are pricelessly revealing in their very reluctance to disclose the famous Audubon secret. Unless we wish to believe that five dear old ladies, his granddaughters, decided to commit a king-size hoax on the world and fabricated the quotations in Maria's little black book, something rather consequential was certainly agitating Audubon all through his life.

Here are a few excerpts from some of the Audubon letters to his wife:

June 4, 1826, At Sea

We are a few miles south of the line for the second time in my life. What ideas it conveys to me of my high birth and the expectations of my younger days.

My high birth, though unknown to the world, was always on my lips, and I felt a pride unbecoming my situation, but I seemed unable to control it.

I am an aristocrat. I cannot divest myself of this knowledge; the feelings it brings remain with me. How can I help this?

Edinburgh 1826 or 1827

Today, as I was shaving, I was struck by my resemblance to my father; not my adopted father but my own father.

October 9, 1828

. . . As I was going to the minister's I thought of my birth, of my curious life, and of the strange incidents that brought me to what I am now known to be. I felt more than once as if *now* was the moment to dispel the cloud; and again I reflected on the consequence, wiped the stream of water that ran cold over my forehead, and concluded to carry my extraordinary secret to the grave. Oh, my Lucy! Oh, my father! Oh! how cruelly situated I am! And yet perhaps it is best that it should be so. I sighed, and walked faster and faster.

Once toward the end of a letter Audubon started to make a statement, then held off, adding, "If I say a few more words, I must put an end to my existence, having forfeited my word of honor and my oath."

Paris, Friday, October 10, 1828

Oh! . . . Lucy, I am quite wild. When young I was easily taught to keep silence and thought nothing of it, but now that I have children myself, children that at one word of mine would rise to eminence and would be—Stop thy pen, or forever be damned, Audubon!

. . . Peaceful woods, to you I must return, and under your dark shades, consecrate my days to the only blessing left me on this earth, that of admiring the works of a Creator who knows who I am, and will repay me for my torments here below.

What might this day have been, if known here? Patient, silent, bashful, and yet powerful of physique and of mind, dressed as a common man, I walk the streets! I bow! I ask permission to do this or that! I follow the publication of a work on natural history that has apparently absorbed my whole knowing life, *I, who should command all!*

I understand now why my father demanded of me a most solemn oath that I should never permit myself to be forced into becoming a priest. I could have had no legitimate heir, and yet that other promise demanded later prevents my sons from ever being known. Cruel! Cruel! but who may foresee the future?

There are several other points which might be mentioned: the likeness of pictures of John James Audubon to those of Marie

Antoinette, and of pictures of the Dauphin to those of Audubon's children; the continued availability, throughout Audubon's life, of the French family of Nicholas Berthaud, always eager to give assistance when Audubon needed it even though his pride kept him from too many appeals to them. "The citizens of Henderson, Kentucky, say that Madame Berthaud was a Lady-in-Waiting to Marie Antoinette," says Mrs. Tyler. And the fact that one Marshal Ney always refused to sit down in the presence of John James Audubon. When asked why, Marshal Ney said significantly, "He is higher than I am! He is higher than Napoleon! He is higher than anybody!"

Oddly enough, according to LeNotre, on the spot where the Temple used to stand in Paris there is now a statue of Diogenes "advancing in the dark, raising his lantern, and, in the obscurity, 'seeking a man.' "

Mrs. Tyler might be challenging the world to help Diogenes in his endeavors as she says, "The great quest of history is to find the man whom that little boy became, a Frenchman, happy, unquenchable, full of life and energy, loving birds passionately, and concealing his own identity from the world."

With such an attractive mystery in his background, is it any wonder that the ghost of Audubon appears when he finds a chance—hoping to inspire someone to search the records and learn the truth about him? He may, of course, continue to travel about a great deal. The habits of a lifetime could hardly change immediately after death. Perhaps he and his birds may still be making beautiful music together in the woods of his beloved America. One cannot help but wonder if there is any history of his ghost being seen at the numerous other houses made famous throughout the country because John James Audubon slept there.

CHAPTER II

𝖨𝖫𝖨𝖫𝖨𝖫𝖨𝖫𝖨𝖫𝖨𝖫

Turbulence
in Toronto

TRIPPING LIGHTLY DOWN the steep staircase at the Mackenzie House in Toronto, accompanied by two tripping hippie
witches, I tripped and nearly fell on my face. At least, I thought
I tripped. Raji said I was pushed by a demon. J.C. insisted it
was an unseen ghost. Whatever it was that was after me knocked
my camera off a table a few minutes later and dented it badly.
I presumed I had just laid the camera carelessly so that it became overbalanced; but Raji said it was pushed by a demon.
J.C. insisted it was an unseen ghost.

Raji and J.C., who had accompanied me to the famous Canadian ghost house, were very nice hippies, but rather an odd
selection for a typically average, square-type woman to go ca-
vorting about with, particularly to haunted houses. That was
partly why I asked them. They were devoutly white (good)
witches (or warlocks, as they prefer to be called); but they were
usually high on grass (marijuana) or hash (hashish), so I really
cannot depend on their testimony at any given time.

It was November 1, 1968, Allhallows. On Halloween I had

flown from Miami (not on a broomstick) to spend All Saints'
Eve with the members of the Celtic-American Church, a cult
of hippie witches. (Oh, I forgot, they don't like to be called
"hippies" because they think that word has a bad connotation.
They prefer the more dated term "hep," or the gentler "flower-
children.")

It was a fascinating experience to participate in their sabbats
and ceremonies, but the discussion of witchcraft in its modern
manifestations will have to wait for another book. It is the ghost
house formerly occupied, and possibly still occupied, by an-
cestors of Canadian Prime Minister William Lyon Mackenzie
King that is inspiring our interest at this moment.

The dark and dismal building at 82 Bond Street in Old Town
is now a national shrine owned and operated by the William
Lyon Mackenzie Homestead Foundation in trust on a nonprofit
basis. But it once housed an active and energetic family. Mackenzie, Toronto's first mayor, was a vigorous and lively man, and
he is now a vigorous and lively ghost, if all reports are to be
believed. It was undoubtedly the haunts in this house that
caused Mackenzie's grandson, the great Canadian statesman, to
become interested in psychical research as early as 1920. Canada
grew into a powerful and prosperous nation during the twenty-
two years that William Lyon Mackenzie King was Prime Minister, and during all that time he kept his secret interest in
psychical phenomena totally guarded from his millions of followers. This was not because he was ashamed of it but because
he thought it might be misunderstood.

Mackenzie King did not want the same thing to happen to
him that had happened to the British Prime Minister W. E.
Gladstone, the Grand Old Man of the Victorian age. Gladstone,
unlike King, had no fear of openly joining the Society for Psychical Research after he became convinced of the actuality of spirit
communication. But the story of a séance he attended went
round the world as spicy gossip, and letters poured in, mainly

from pious people who were horrified at seeing him engaged in "sorcery" or else anxious to save him from becoming the victim of imposture.

Gladstone, like another British Prime Minister, the first Earl of Balfour, who committed himself even further on the subject, was not deterred. He was thoroughly convinced that the research he was engaged in was good and worthy. Balfour became interested through his sister, who was the wife of Professor Henry Sidgwick of Cambridge University, the first president of the Society for Psychical Research; and in 1894 Balfour also became president of this learned group.

Mackenzie King, however, said in a letter to the late psychiatrist and parapsychologist Dr. Nandor Fodor, "It does not seem advisable to become too actively identified with psychical research in the public mind." In *Between Two Worlds* Fodor quotes another letter to him from King expressing his interest in a certain book. It reads, "The parts of the book which had to do with evidences of personal survival, also of teachings, appealed very strongly to me, and were in the nature of confirmation of experiences of my own concern, of which there can be no doubt whatever."

Among the experiences he referred to was one involving a prediction of a death. Mackenzie King, a lonely and sorely bereaved man in later years, had a tremendous fondness for his dog Pat. I should say his dogs Pat. The incident involves the first of three dogs he had, all named Pat. He often told of the premonitory experience he had the night before the first Pat died. His watch fell off his bedside table for no apparent reason and was found in the morning face down on the floor, the hands stopped at 4:20. King said, "I am not psychic, but I knew then, as if a voice were speaking to me, that Pat would die before another twenty-four hours went by." The prediction was fulfilled. That night Pat climbed out of his basket with a last effort and died on his master's bed. The time was exactly 4:20.

While the Prime Minister did not mind sharing stories such

as this about his own personal experiences with those he knew
would understand, he carefully protected his reputation by not
allowing them to become publicized until after his death in 1950.
Since then his psychical interests have been reported in several
publications.

His grandfather, William Lyon Mackenzie, was born in Dun-
dee, Scotland, in 1795 and later emigrated to Canada where he
became a shopkeeper at the town of York (now Toronto). Always a rebel, he founded a newspaper named *The Colonial
Advocate,* in which his fiery attacks on the governing clique
made him a political hero. He was elected to the Legislative
Assembly of Upper Canada in 1828 and re-elected five times. In
1834 he became mayor of Toronto's first civic government. A
fighter all the way, it is since his death in 1861 in his house on
Bond Street that he has rebelled the most—against the con-
formity of resting peacefully in his grave.

For a while after Mackenzie's death one of his daughters had
a girls' school in the house on Bond Street. His daughter Isabel
Grace, who was a slim eighteen-year-old when her father died,
later married and became the mother of Prime Minister William
Lyon Mackenzie King.

Fate magazine, January 1961, and the Toronto *Telegram,*
whose reporter Andrew MacFarlane took the signed depositions
of several witnesses to ghostly activities in the house, have given
us a complete report of them. MacFarlane indicates clearly why
the caretaker's flat on the top floor of the house, although comfortable and in excellent condition, was empty when I was there
and closed off from the public. Nobody will live there. The
curator just comes in the morning, spends the day, and returns
home at night to her own safe little nest. That is the only way
to do it, really!

The house itself is small—actually it must have been one of a
row of houses all joined together at one time, for it is narrow,
as such structures always are. It is only the width of one room
and a hallway. Each floor has only two main rooms, one in back

of the other. On the ground floor there is a kitchen at the front and a family dining room behind it, more like what we would today use as a breakfast room. On the first floor, where the front entrance opens into the hall, there is a parlor, much too dressy and prim to be called a living room. In it there is a steeplechase clock under a glass bell. There are cracking oil portraits on the walls, the most interesting being that of William Lyon Mackenzie himself in all his mayoral dignity. On a table with a tasseled velvet tablecloth a family album shows faces of people long since dead framed in lozenge-shaped depressions in its heavy pages. In one corner a small antique piano stands in silence— in the daytime. It has often been heard playing at night after the house was locked and the caretaker's family had retired upstairs.

I posed Raji the warlock with his hands in the air over the keys of this piano to feel the vibrations from it—and he said he felt very peculiar ones—and the Polaroid picture I snapped reveals a mysterious kind of mist between his hands and the keys. If this was caused by a double exposure, why is not the rest of the picture in duplicate? Yes, you can take a double exposure with a Polaroid if you snap the shutter twice. I just do not quite see how I got the effect I did, even if it *had* been a double exposure.

Back of the living room on that floor is a formal dining room, and I particularly noticed the important position given to a picture of a dog. Wonder which of the famous Pats that is. On the floor above are two bedrooms. The entire house is furnished with antiques, but all are separated from the halls by partitions so that the public cannot reach them, touch them, and sneak mementos from them. I am told the human souvenir hunter is more destructive than ghosts in famous haunted houses.

There has recently been a large addition constructed at the back of the first floor. It contains a modern kitchen and a room that holds some of William Lyon Mackenzie's favorite objects. The printing press he bought in 1825, which is locked but still in working order, the scarred wooden desk Mackenzie used when he was a member of the Legislative Assembly in 1826, and the red leather chair in which he sat as the city's first mayor are all there. These used to reside in the cellar until this addition was built to house them. It was from the cellar that the sounds of the locked printing press in operation used to be heard at night.

Footsteps have been heard, too, on many occasions. These things tend to discourage anyone from wanting to live in that top-floor apartment.

Let us go now to the testimony detailed in sworn affidavits from those people who innocently accepted the job of caretaker and blithely moved their belongings up the three flights of stairs and settled down for what they thought would be lengthy tenures. Mr. and Mrs. Alex Dobban moved into the apartment in April 1960, but they stayed only one month. Mr. Dobban had retired on a pension from a maintenance job in a downtown Toronto office building, and taking care of the Mackenzie House seemed like an ideal arrangement for them. They got the flat rent free and a small salary to supplement his pension and the whole setup just looked great. Until Mrs. Dobban's nerves went to pieces because of all the commotion in the night.

Her story started, "We hadn't been here long when I heard footsteps going up the stairs. I called to my husband, but he wasn't there. There was no one else in the house—but I definitely heard feet on the stairs.

"One night I woke up. There was a rumbling noise in the basement. At first I took it to be the oil burner; but my husband checked and the furnace wasn't on. As it turned out, the noise I heard was the press. It's locked, but I heard it running, not only that night but one or two other nights as well."

Mrs. Dobban reported that on another night she heard the piano in the front room downstairs playing after they were in bed. There was no one else in the house but the piano was playing. It was not a tune. It was more as if someone were hitting the keys with closed fists, or a child were playing at the piano.

Mrs. Dobban did not believe in ghosts, but she began to suspect that the house was haunted. Neither she nor her husband had picked up any rumors about it before that time. Mr. Dobban did not hear any of the sounds that worried his wife so much. He must have been an unusually sound sleeper. But he believed his wife and so they went away from there. But spooks? Said Mrs. Dobban, "How else can you explain it?"

Mr. and Mrs. Charles Edmunds had survived the anxieties of nights in the Mackenzie House for over three years before they gave up the ghost. They moved there on August 13, 1956, and stuck it out until April 1960. The Dobbans were hired to take their place. Because they were embarrassed to talk about the things they had undergone in the house, the Edmunds kept what they saw and heard to themselves for the most part. When they finally unloaded to the Toronto *Telegram*, though, they had a story-and-a-half to tell.

As the tension mounted during those three years, Mrs. Edmunds lost almost forty pounds. It was that constant, oppressive presence of something, they did not know what, that finally drove them out of their comfortable, rent-free quarters. Footsteps on the stairs were heard from their very first day in the house, and they continued to occur nearly every day when there was nobody about who could have caused them physically. Then the haunting got worse. Mrs. Edmunds reported:

"One night I woke up at midnight to see a lady standing over my bed. She wasn't at the side, but at the head of the bed, leaning over me. There is no room for anyone to stand where she was. The bed is pushed up against the wall. She was hanging down, like a shadow, but I could see her clearly. Something seemed to touch me on the shoulder to wake me up. She had long hair hanging down in front of her shoulders, dark brown, I think. She had a long narrow face. Then she was gone.

"Two years ago, early in March, I saw the lady again. It was the same—except this time she reached out and hit me. When I got up in the morning my left eye was purple and bloodshot."

Mrs. Edmunds also saw a little man at night every once in a while. He was bald and wore a frock coat. She would see him for just a few seconds and then he would vanish. She often saw either that man or the woman standing in the room—at least eight or nine times in all.

Charles Edmunds is a Royal Army pensioner who says he does not believe in the supernatural. Yet, he said, "Certain happenings during the three years and eight months my wife and I served as caretakers of the Mackenzie Homestead have convinced me that there is something peculiar about the place." The little man his wife saw is one of the most peculiar—because he brought evidence. We are always looking for evidence of their identity from ghosts, wherever possible.

Mr. Edmunds said, "On one occasion my wife and I were sleeping in the upstairs bedroom. She woke me up in the middle of the night and said that she had seen a man standing beside her bed. My wife, to my certain knowledge, knew nothing of Mackenzie or his history. All of the pictures in the homestead show Mackenzie as a man with hair on his head. The man my wife saw and described to me was completely bald with side whiskers. I had read about Mackenzie. He wore a wig to cover his baldness. But she did not know this."

Mrs. Edmunds said that sometimes when they were sitting watching television her husband might look up all of a sudden at the doorway. "I knew what it was," she said. "You felt that someone had just come in."

The lady's report stated that she had felt the homestead shaking with a rumbling noise some nights. They thought at first it might be the subway, but reasoned it out that they were too far from the subway to feel the vibrations. They ultimately decided it was the printing press running in the basement—that printing press which was always kept locked.

Mrs. Edmunds' concluding statement was very fair. There is no use being mad at a haunt, after all. It won't get you anywhere. She said, "I did not believe in ghosts when I went to stay at the

Mackenzie Homestead. But I do now. It's the only explanation I can think of. I wish to say that I would not say anything against the Mackenzies. They were hard-working people and so are we. They were not hard on us. It's just that the house was a strain on the nerves."

Mr. Edmunds recalled an incident involving his two grandchildren. His son Robert and Robert's wife and children stayed with them for a time and became involved in the ghostly activities. He said, "Susan [then aged four] and Ronnie [then aged three] went from the upstairs bedroom down to the second-floor bathroom at night. A few minutes later there were terrific screams. I went down and they were both huddled in the bathroom, terrified. They said there was a lady in the bathroom. I asked where she was now and they said she just disappeared.

"On another night my wife woke up screaming. She said, 'There was a small man standing over the bed.' She described Mackenzie. Another night, a woman came up to the bed and looked at my missus. She was a little woman, about my wife's height. My wife said, 'Dad, there was a woman here.' I told her she was dreaming.

"Another night my wife woke up and woke me. She was upset. She said the lady had hit her. There were three red welts on the left side of her face. They were like finger marks. The next day her eye was bloodshot. Then it turned black and blue. Something had hit her. It wasn't me. I don't think she could have done it herself. And there wasn't anyone else in the house."

Mr. Edmunds described another occasion on which something peculiar happened to some flowers they had in pots on a window ledge inside the house. "This was in winter and we had the geraniums inside. We water the plants twice a week, on Sundays and Wednesdays. On a Saturday morning we found that they all had been watered, although we hadn't done it. There was water spilled all over the plants and the saucers they were standing in were full. There was mud on the curtains and holes in the earth as if someone had poked their fingers in. There was water on the dressing table. Neither of us had watered the plants and neither had anyone else."

Mr. Edmunds testified to having also heard the footsteps on the stairs that so bothered his wife. "They were thumping footsteps like someone with heavy boots. This happened frequently when there was no one in the house but us, when we were sitting together upstairs."

"The whole house used to shake with a rumbling sound sometimes," Mr. Edmunds verified his wife's account here too. He concluded his testimony: "I am not an imaginative man and I do not believe in ghosts. But the fact is that the house was strange enough so that we had to leave. We would have stayed if it had not been for these happenings. But my wife could not stand it any longer."

Robert and Minnie Edmunds also made sworn statements about their experiences. He said that his wife woke him one night, saying that she heard the piano playing downstairs. "I heard it, too," he said. "I cannot remember what the music was like, but it was the piano downstairs playing."

Robert's wife woke him another night to say that the printing press in the basement was running. The young man heard the sound also and described it as a rumbling, clanking noise like the old presses he had seen in movies and on television—"not like modern presses," he said. Robert and Minnie only heard this press run once, but they heard the piano play three or four times.

Robert Edmunds ended his statement with that same routine old saw to the effect that he previously did not believe in ghosts *but* . . . "I find it hard to explain what we heard."

Minnie's statement was, "I can think of no natural explanation for these occurrences."

I was bravely willing to spend a night in this house with a bunch of my hippie witches, if it had been allowed. But I could easily understand why the Homestead Foundation refused to break its ruling to allow me to do so. It had become the popular

Halloween indoor sport in Toronto for groups to go there to spend the night, hoping to observe a ghost or two. The Foundation had to make new rulings and be firm about them, and an author arriving suddenly on Halloween could hardly hope to have red tape scissored on short notice. Anyhow, the way I seemed to be pushed around during my daylight visit, it is probably just as well I was not there at night.

Reporter Andy MacFarlane had been allowed to spend the night in the haunted house in June 1960, because it was not yet forbidden at that time. Accompanied by photographer Joe Black, MacFarlane took his typical newspaper skepticism with him; and, as so often happens to the skeptics, nothing happened. This is what makes them so sure that those who proclaim genuine experiences on other occasions are deluded.

The two newspaper men entered the house a few minutes before midnight and had an uncomfortable moment right away when their flashlight picked up the life-size effigy of a woman in period dress that was standing in the parlor. They turned on the lights quickly, and for the rest of the night they did not get out of sight of each other. They toured the old house, then they clicked off the parlor lights and sat on the antique and lumpy upholstery of the sofa to await developments that never came.

Nothing happened and they saw no trace of ghost or ghoul. They heard not a single unaccountable footfall. The stairs did not even creak. Eventually both men fell asleep and did not awaken until dawn. Had spooks played tic-tac-toe on their cheekbones for the rest of the night, they would never have known.

On the night of July 1, 1960, Archdeacon John Frank of Holy Trinity Church conducted an ancient exorcism service in the Mackenzie Homestead. The prayer that the Archdeacon read to exorcise the ghosts came from the service of complin in the new Anglican prayer book. It reads: "The Lord Almighty granteth a quiet night and a perfect end. O God, make speed to save us; O Lord, make haste to help us. . . . Visit, we beseech Thee, O

Lord, this place and drive from it all the snares of the enemy; let Thy holy angels dwell herein to preserve us in peace. . . . Look down, O Lord, from Thy heavenly throne, illuminate the darkness of this night with Thy celestial brightness, and from the sons of light banish the deeds of darkness; through Jesus Christ our Lord. Amen."

Perhaps this exorcism has been successful in helping the restless spirits of the Mackenzie Homestead find peace. It has been over one hundred years since William Lyon Mackenzie died, and he surely deserves a little peace and quiet by now. So does his busy house.

If Mackenzie does not still make ethereal nightly visits, however, someone else does, according to my latest report. An attractive young lady named Wendy, who was not a witch and not a hippie or heppie or flower child or whatever, and who definitely was not tripping on drugs or dope of any kind, gave me a clear-cut account of her visit to the house. Just the year before I was in Toronto six young people, three boys and three girls, managed to get special permission to spend the night in the homestead because, Wendy said, "one of my friends knew someone that runs the place."

The young people wandered all over the house at first and then they settled down on the floor of the second-story back bedroom and waited quietly for something to happen, all the while telling ghost stories and getting themselves in a properly receptive mood.

"We figured if anything was going to happen it would happen around midnight," Wendy said, "but nothing did. Time dragged on and then it was one o'clock, and we felt a draft. None of the windows was open or anything, so there was no reason for a draft, but there it was. Then we just sort of saw this misty type of figure. We couldn't make it out too well but it looked more or less like the form of a man. It just sort of appeared. It didn't come through the wall or anything. It was just there, all of a sudden."

Of course, Mr. Mackenzie or his wife, or even one of his daughters, might have decided to materialize once more and made it only part way—into a misty figure instead of an exact replica of his former body. Then again, and this seems more likely to me, this could be a good example of the type of ghost I spoke about in the Preface, that is actually caused by the fears and anticipations of the persons assembled for the specific purpose of seeing a ghost and getting shivers of excitement from it. I cannot say exactly how this could work, and what physical processes would cause it to happen; but it seems to me to be the logical explanation. However it was caused, it served its purpose and badly frightened a group of receptive young people.

"It was really weird," says Wendy. "We were scared. We got out of there pretty fast."

CHAPTER III

Shades of Rosemary's Baby!

A DIVERTISSEMENT AS engaging as those presented on television by producer Gary Smith was performed in his own home in the dark and gargoyled Dakota apartments just before he moved in. Its star was a ghost.

Those who saw the movie *Rosemary's Baby* are familiar with the glowering Dakota because it was the scene of that bedeviled witchery. It was also the inspiration for the setting of the book by Ira Levin from which the movie was made. This enormous, fortresslike edifice was originally constructed in 1884 on the corner of 72nd Street and Central Park West as one of New York's earliest luxury apartment buildings. It proudly boasted one of the first elevators ever used, even though it was so far from the then fashionable living areas of the city that naming it for the Dakota Territory seemed an ironic witticism.

Although from the look of it the Dakota might have been built for the denning of ghosts and witches, it actually was constructed to order for Edward Clark, president of the Singer Sewing Machine Company, to be the home of the executives of his company. History does not record how it worked out to have all the top employees—and their families!—under one roof; but I notice the practice did not last long. Since then a variety of celebrities and ordinary citizens have lived at the Dakota, impressed by the Victorian magnificence of its apartments, the elegant fireplaces, the immense mirrors, the high ceilings—and the high rents! I am sure those who reside there also appreciate the fact that the structure, built on a square with a courtyard in the center, has heavy iron gates protecting their property. Not even witches can pass in the night without giving the countersign.

To reach Gary Smith's apartment, once you have withstood the scrutiny of the guard, you go into the courtyard through the gateway and walk alongside the wall to the left until you enter a dark-paneled hallway. Here you step into a large elevator with wall-to-wall mirrors and brass hand rails all around; and just for the fun of it you seat yourself on one of the cushioned benches as you rise to your floor. Almost reluctantly you leave the gleaming comforts of the elevator when you reach seven, then walk around to the right of it and ring the bell on the door of number seventy-seven.

This is what Norvin Malone did one day in the late fall of 1965 as he went to join two friends who had been hired to refinish the apartment before Smith and his family took possession. Norvin is a market researcher by profession and planned to do the manual work evenings and weekends to make some extra money for Christmas. When Frank Andrews opened the door for Norvin, the young man stepped into a large square hall—everything in that building is either large or square, or both. He also stepped into one of the most interesting experiences of his life, for here he was to encounter his first ghost.

The apartment had belonged to actress Judy Holliday, and that lovely and talented lady had just died of cancer. She had been ill a long, long time before her death, and her home had developed a complexion of somber and dingy unhappiness. Even the walls, which in the bare expanses of space seemed to stretch endlessly toward the ceilings, were painted gray or else were covered with wallpaper of subdued tone and remote patterns. All the massive woodwork was dark mahogany. The kitchen, for some unknown reason, was papered and painted entirely in black, adding to the gloomy effect the entire apartment had on Norvin from the moment he entered.

Frank Andrews and Ray Johnston had already been at work there day and night for some time. Their goal was to refinish the floors, walls, and fittings in time for the Smiths to move in by Thanksgiving. Norvin was set to work at first scrubbing and burnishing the endless amount of brass in the apartment. As he polished up the handle of the big front door, he was told a few more or less relevant details about his new locale of employment, including the fact that it seemed to have a ghost. No specter had as yet actually been seen, but an unembodied presence was strongly felt, Frank and Ray reported.

Norvin's reaction on hearing this was to bring his Ouija board to work with him the next night. The boys realized that Ouijas are notoriously unreliable and so they did not put much stock in what it revealed to them. Yet its statements oddly resembled and confirmed the adventures they were soon to have.

Sitting flat on the floor in one of the two small back bedrooms, with the board between them, Frank and Norvin put their hands on the pointer while Ray wrote down the message that was spelled out. They thus learned that, yes, their feelings of a "presence" had been correct. There was an entity in residence who resented their efforts to paint his bedroom. Apparently if it had been good enough for him alive, it was good enough for him dead. Who was he? He gave a name that the boys do not remember, and he stated that he had lived in that apartment.

These young men were remarkably casual about all this. It is wise to be that way with Ouija boards until they give you documentable evidence; yet one wonders why Frank or Norvin did not find it of interest to try to learn if they were receiving anything of an evidential nature. They could have made an effort to verify the name they received, to learn if it were actually that of a former tenant. But instead, they forgot it. The truth is, I presume, that since they had not yet seen their ghost, they did not take him too seriously at the time.

"I didn't have any feeling about the apartment," Norvin told me, "except that it was inhabited. I felt vibrations, that's all." Frank Andrews had noticed something too large to be a rat scurrying down the halls from time to time since he had been there. "It didn't have any form," he says, so he paid little attention to it, except to tell Ray, and Norvin when he came, that it was there. The thing that impressed Frank more than anything else about his experience in the Dakota was the similarities in his own life and *Rosemary's Baby*. In the first place, the apartment in the book was number seven, and here he was working in number seventy-seven. In the second place, the girls in the book are named Rosemary and Terry, and Frank has two sisters whose names are Rosemary and Terry. Also, Frank has been interested in witchcraft for some time. He thinks such coincidences as these are more interesting than ghosts. Frank also found it impressive that Boris Karloff lived in the Dakota at that time.

Then one day Frank Andrews really saw the ghost, and his interest changed somewhat. "I got a good look at it," he said. "It was standing to the side of me watching me paint. It was a boy around nine or ten years old, not yet a teenager, I would say. It gave off a strange outdoorsy, fresh-yet-musty odor. It wore the costume of another era—little short pants, jacket, and vest."

After the ghost watched Frank work for a while it ambled off down the hall and into the second bedroom, one of the two now used as Gary Smith's children's rooms.

It is odd that Frank saw a child ghost, yet it appeared to Norvin as a young man. The similarity of its actions would make it seem to be the same ghost, yet it manifested itself differently to the two persons who saw it. This curious discrepancy in a way somehow gives more veracity to the two independent testimonies. Otherwise one might suspect the young men of having fabricated a story of a haunting just because they felt it appropriate to the Dakota in which they were working.

It was daylight when Norvin first saw the apparition. He says, "It was standing in the hall looking at me through the huge double doors which I had thrown open while I was painting in the living room. I felt someone staring at me and glanced up out of the corner of my eye. It was about ten to fifteen feet away from me, watching me curiously. After about a minute I decided to look directly at it and it vanished. I continued to paint."

Asked to describe his ghost, Norvin said, "He may have been in his twenties but he had such a childish face it's hard to tell. He must have been retarded because he looked so young he gave the impression of being no more than three or four years old. But he was too tall for that. He had brownish wavy hair, long, but not long like the hippies wear theirs. He was dressed in a period costume close to Edwardian. Foppish but not terribly so. Formal. The coat was almost like a smoking jacket. He wore a white shirt with a dark bow tie—a big tie, like artists wear."

In contrast, when they compare notes, Frank insists that he definitely saw a child. He remembers him vividly and, he says, "If it was a man he would have had to be a midget."

About a week later Norvin had been out shopping for the lunches the youths usually ate together sitting on the floor. Frank was alone refinishing the floor in the immense dining room. Norvin said, "He didn't hear me return through the front door and the hall had been carpeted by then. So I tiptoed down the hall and into the dining room and quietly crept up on Frank and grabbed him. He screamed, of course, because he thought it was the ghost. 'He's been standing at the hall door watching me,' he said. 'When you jumped me I decided maybe he'd reached the point of trying to do something to stop us.'"

The only thing the ghost ever did to harm anyone occurred

one day after the Smiths' furniture had begun to arrive. Frank was standing on a ladder painting the inside of the big walk-in closet off the master bedroom. The door closed itself and the light went out automatically.

"I'm not too scared by these things, actually," Frank said. "I got down off the ladder and propped the door open with a chair so it wouldn't close again. I climbed back up the ladder and was reaching up painting the ceiling when my arm went down against the bare light bulb that was in a fixed position over the door. It remained there just as if someone had pulled it down there and was holding it. I was so startled I just watched my skin being charred. I finally jerked it away, but not until I had a burn about six inches above the wrist on the underside of my arm. Oddly enough, I didn't feel any pain at the time or later." But he still has the scar from the burn.

Frank was angry at the indignity of this personal attack from an entity he had encountered with no animosity until then. "It's got to go," he declared. He told me later, "I know something about magic and so I did some magic. The ghost disappeared for several weeks."

Perhaps it was because they wanted to check on their own powers of observation, perhaps because they were aware that the less they told each other, the more veracity their accounts of the supernormal happenings would have. Whatever the reason, the boys were very cagey when they discussed the reappearance of the entity.

"I didn't mention it to Norvin or Ray," Frank says, "but I began to be aware of its presence again. This time I felt it strongly in the hallway. Then Norvin said to me one day, 'It's back.'

" 'I know,' I answered. 'Where is it?' "

" 'In the hallway.' After that we saw it off and on in different places in the apartment."

Thanksgiving came and went and the work in number seventy-seven was not complete, but the Smith family moved in anyway. And the ghost moved out once again.

"Frank, it's gone," Norvin said. Frank nodded. He had put no magic curse on it this time so he did not know why or how it had disappeared. But they both were sure that the creepy feeling of its presence was no longer there.

"Then," Norvin told me, "one day I was walking down the hall and looked into the bedroom where the haunt had been in the first place. It was furnished by then and was the bedroom of the Smiths' little girl. There was a huge stuffed dog—about three feet high—sitting at the foot of the bed on its haunches. Its front feet were straight. Suddenly I became aware that the entity had gone into the dog and was living in it. That was the best choice it could make around there. The live dog in this family was a Yorkshire terrier and nothing in its right mind would have inhabited that animal!"

When I met this little Yorkshire later I coudn't have agreed with Norvin less. I thought Winston was most personable. But then, everyone has a right to his own opinion. "Live and let live" should apply to dogs as well as ghosts.

Norvin said, "I went to Frank and told him, 'I've found him. He's back.'

" 'Yes,' he said, 'I know.'

"I said, 'Where is he?'

"He replied, 'He's in the stuffed animal in the girl's room.' So once again we verified each other."

Frank reports that he saw an aura of lights around the dog or tiger or whatever the animal was, he was not sure of its species. They were lights or emanations that he did not feel would have been there unless something human—or previously human—were inhabiting it. He also got that unusual odor from the animal that he always smelled when the ghost appeared.

Norvin added, "One day later I was talking to Mrs. Smith. Her children at the time were rolling and tumbling on the floor with the stuffed dog, and I said to her, 'They certainly enjoy playing with the dog.' Mrs. Smith replied, 'It's very strange but at the other place where we lived before the children would not play with that toy. It wasn't until we moved to the Dakota that they have taken it up so enthusiastically.'

"I laughed," said Norvin, "and went on out of the room. We had never told them anything about the ghost. Ray had sensed it, but I am not sure he had seen it. He acknowledges psychic things but prefers to live in strict substantiality and ignore the peripheral areas of psychical phenomena. So he had warned us not to mention it to the Smiths."

It is pleasant to think of a childish ghost finding a comfortable sanctuary in a stuffed animal and remaining there to play with the offspring in a busy family. When I called on the Smiths a year later and was shown around the lovely apartment, I made it a special point to look for such a large cloth-covered pet. I doubted that I would be able to see any aura or glint in its eye that might inform me if it were inhabited, but I looked nonetheless. However, although there were many stuffed animals and toys of all kinds in the children's rooms, there was none so large that it answered the description I had been given of the ghost's abode.

Maybe Frank is right in his conjecture that it did not stay around there long. He told me that before all the work was finished and he and Ray were ready to leave he had seen the ghost for the last time. It was proceeding down the long central hall, walking rather slowly, with back erect, and definitely not scurrying as usual. Frank was impelled by the realization that the entity was walking toward the front door with the intention of leaving the place forever.

When the ghost left, it is to be hoped that he took with him from the apartment all remnants of unhappiness. According to Judy Holliday's mother, Mrs. Helen Tuvim, "All of her troubles happened in *that* apartment. I can't even look at it. She got her divorce there. She got her cancer there."

But her mother is sure that Judy Holliday had never seen the ghost. The actress did apparently have a clairvoyant streak, however. Her mother told me she would often say, "Oh, I knew that was going to happen! I must be psychic!" She was superstitious, too, as many theater people are, and afraid to face unpleasant facts, according to Mrs. Tuvim.

Judy lived in number seventy-seven for sixteen years. Her mother moved in with her and remained there until the star died. Now Mrs. Tuvim lives in an apartment a block away and teaches music. She does not believe in ghosts, or in the possibility of being psychic, or anything else of that "superstitious" nature. Yet she was eager to tell me what had occurred the same night that I first contacted her. Judy's son Jonathan at that time attended boardingschool in Massachusetts. He never wrote to his grandmother, but on rare occasions they would get lonesome for one another and talk on the telephone. That evening, Helen Tuvim said, "I was going to call him and as I put my hand on the phone the bell rang. It was him calling me." She felt there might be something more than coincidence that shortly after she had this possibly ESP experience with Jonathan I had telephoned her—to ask her about Judy Holliday and her psychic interests. Since Mrs. Tuvim could recall no other evidence of ESP in her lifetime, it seemed to her more than chance that the subject should be illustrated for her just before she was called upon to discuss it.

Mrs. Tuvim is an elderly woman whose grief for her daughter is pathetic because she has no faith and no hope of ever seeing her again. One is tempted to wish her many more psychic experiences in order that they might somehow give her comfort.

Gary Smith, an inventive, talented, and interesting man with a mop of curly hair, has imbued the apartment now with a vigor and liveliness that should make short shrift of any unhappy memories that may still exist there. His attractive wife, Gail, and their three active children, Daisy, age seven, Douglas, age five, and Sam, two—born after they moved to the Dakota—keep the place buzzing like a newspaper office on press day. Winston, the Yorkshire terrier, and the five cats over whom he presides, are into every nook and cranny. They would surely poke out a ghost in short order, and perhaps they have.

One cat, Phoebe, acted as if I were her favorite brand of catnip, clinging to me, sitting on my lap, and demanding so much loving attention that I became suspicious of her. If a male ghost were seeking a hiding place in a house, what cozier place could he reside than in this cat? That might also explain his taking on so over a female visitor. But Gary assured me that Phoebe has been that way all the eleven years of her life, only the last four of which have been spent at number seventy-seven, the Dakota.

Gail Smith not only oversees the care of her children and the house, plus one in Southampton in the summer, but she is an amateur gardener. The butler's pantry there is full of cuttings and rootings; and pots of ferns, ivy, dieffenbachia, and philodendron are all over the house. I must exclaim over what an absolutely delightful and charming place the apartment now is. The decorator who restored it has used what might be called a Victorian-modern decor, accenting the best of two extremes. Keeping intact all the priceless fireplaces with the large mirrors over them, and the exquisite molding, he has added contemporary wallpaper and painting techniques with most effective results. The ceiling in the library, for instance, is painted a deep, brilliant blue. The first strip of molding around the edge of it is a vivid green. The center space, about six inches deep, has a soft red patterned wallpaper, and there is another strip of green molding below it. The whole effect is warm and modern, yet the room's marble fireplace with its mirror reaching to the ceiling adds opulence and dignity.

The huge dining room is now a den or playroom, with wild wallpaper of bright blue-and-white check or plaid. A billiard table the size of a house trailer takes up much of the middle space. A television set has been mounted into the wall over the fireplace. The walls are covered with photographs of Gary Smith standing beside the famous stars with whom he has worked, such as Barbra Streisand, "Satchmo" Armstrong, Dinah Shore, Trini Lopez, and many others. Smith is the producer of the Kraft Music Hall television series. Among many others, he has done the Barbra Streisand spectaculars, "Hullabaloo," and recently that delightful hour of Gordon Jenkins music called "What It Was, Was Love" sung by Steve Lawrence and Eydie Gorme.

Gary Smith likes poster art and there is much of that around; but his *pièces de résistance* he has painted himself, using oils in halftone dots in the printing technique of photographic reproduction. It is most effective. His hobby, he admits, is painting rather abstract art in a modern representational manner. He was an art director and scenic designer for theater and television before becoming a television director.

Oddly enough, although Ray Johnston was the one who had warned the boys who worked there not to talk about the ghost, it is apparently he who told the Smiths that something spooky had been going on there. Both Frank and Norvin assured me that they did not know anything about their ghost, yet Gail Smith said, "The boys who worked here before we moved in told me they had felt the presence of a friendly ghost who seemed to be waiting around to decide what we were going to do with the house."

Mrs. Smith thinks she is a bit psychic herself, but she has never seen any evidence of any haunting of her new apartment. As vivaciously as it is now decorated, and as full as it is of rambunctious children and animals, a phantom could hardly find any of the peace and quiet he surely would need in order to lurk about in corners and closets. After the stuffed animal was removed, the ghost evidently must have eliminated himself also. Or perhaps when Frank saw him stalking up the hall with all that dignity, he was making his spectral farewell to an apartment to which he had been attached, but which he now evidently realized to be untenable—for ghosts.

Yes, I think it can safely be said that when a busy executive and his wife, three very young children, one Yorkshire terrier, and five cats move into an apartment—even one in the Dakota—the ghost goes out the window.

CHAPTER IV

The Ghost of
the San Marcos Bridge

ONE WOULD HARDLY expect to have a bit of Texas folklore corroborated by a hard-headed modern businessman and several army personnel; but this story has been verified as fact by a number of such individuals who had no possible plans to see a ghost when they crossed the San Marcos Bridge.

Roy Pennycuick, a professor of economics at St. Mary's College, San Antonio, had his weird experience back in 1939, at a time when he was employed by General Motors Acceptance Corporation and had been making collections for them in South Texas.

One Saturday night in September of that year Pennycuick and a companion named Graham were traveling with $25,000 in currency in their car. They were naturally more than somewhat apprehensive because of it, but hardly enough to conjure up a ghost from their imaginations. A payment on a fleet of trucks had been made in cash after the banks had closed that afternoon, and so these men were driving as quickly as possible to reach a State Police Headquarters where they could leave the money in a safe until Monday morning. They were on a back road between Nixon and San Marcos, a small town forty-seven miles north of San Antonio. While crossing a rickety old bridge over the San Marcos River, the car had a flat. One can share with them the suspense of getting out at night on a deserted road to fix a tire, knowing they could be relieved of $25,000 at any moment. It was not the most comfortable situation to be in.

While repairing the flat both men looked up to find a stranger staring fixedly at them, and grinning an outlandish, snaggle-toothed grin. He never said a word in response to any of their queries; but he remained there for some ten minutes. Then he disappeared as abruptly and unaccountably as he had appeared. They did not see him go, but suddenly he just was not there any more.

During the period of time Roy had his visitor under observation he was able to memorize his description. He was as real and solid as any man of bone and skin, and so there was never any suggestion that he might be a ghost in the mind of either man who saw him. He wore flat-heeled old-style black infantry boots and gray trousers such as were used by Southern soldiers in the Civil War. He had no shirt, and his undershirt was the old-fashioned short-sleeved slip-on style with three buttons at the neck. Over it were black suspenders. On his head he wore a Confederate Army cap.

The man was tall, slender, and stoop-shouldered, and he was leaning on a gun. This was a muzzle-loading Kentucky long Tom rifle, probably the fifty-two-inch length. Its stock was resting on the ground and the stranger had his hands cupped over the muzzle. On them he rested his chin—as he stared at the men, grinning his gap-toothed grin and saying not a word.

The fact that this gentleman was gun-equipped made Roy sidle up to the front seat of the car and reach for his revolver, which he tucked in his belt. Then he returned to query the visitor and try to make him tell who he was and what he wanted with them. When he did not respond, they resumed their work on the tire. The next time they looked up their observer was no longer with them; but where or when he went they did not know.

When you have seen an entity costumed for the War between the States, who appears and disappears suddenly without explanation and does not speak to you, you are inclined to pass him off as some neighborhood kook. You certainly never would suspect him to be an apparition. It was not until several weeks later that this idea was suggested to Roy Pennycuick. Back home in Lockhart, Texas, Roy mentioned his queer experience to Pat King, with whom he lived. Pat laughed and said, "Why, you saw the San Marcos Bridge Ghost, that's all." With this explanation, which was no explanation at all, Roy's experience rested for a long time. He thought about it only occasionally until it was oddly confirmed for him at a party in San Antonio some years later.

That night Roy Pennycuick met Lt. Col. Scott Townsend, who gave him the entire historical background of his ghost and corroborated his experience. As provost marshal in World War II, deploying soldiers between San Antonio and Bastrop, Col. Townsend heard a number of men who had to cross the bridge on the San Marcos-Nixon Highway speak of seeing the ghost. He eventually heard so much about it that he did some research on it. This urge was encouraged when Col. Townsend himself saw the entity. After that he interviewed many others who had seen it and took their testimony. He also learned the local legend involving this apparition—which, Roy decided, turns out to be much more than a mere folk story when confirmed by modern military men who witnessed it.

The story is that two brothers who lived in a small house (reportedly still extant at this writing) by the bridge over the San Marcos River were called to enlist in the Civil War. They swore to return dead or alive. One was killed in battle, but he did not let a little thing like that keep him from following his resolution to return . . . and return . . . and return.

If the little weatherworn and almost tumbledown shack still retains one phantom who makes regular sorties on the bridge, perhaps it has his brother also. Roy Pennycuick does not intend to try to find out. What he saw was evidence enough for any one man. He knew something mighty peculiar stood and stared at him for ten minutes, and it has since been identified for him on excellent authority as a ghost. As far as he is concerned, that settles it.

CHAPTER V

The Doctor's Dilemma

ABOUT THE SUREST way to convince a physician of the existence of ghosts is to put one in his house. If you can arrange for several entities, complete with moans and groans, to live around the place for years—depend on it, you have got yourself a puzzled doctor. Such a one is Dr. Kendall D. Gregory, a prominent internist of Gulfport, Mississippi, who has been living in a very haunted house since 1957. It was not until about 1963 that the family finally allowed itself to be convinced that it might really have ghosts; but since then so much has happened that there is no doubt in anyone's mind. Not even Dr. Gregory's.

M.D.'s are notoriously cynical as regards the possibility of evidence of an afterlife, and Gregory even now is careful not to go too far in admitting how much his beliefs have been altered because of his experience; yet he discusses freely what he has seen and heard in the house. That moan he surrounded, for instance.

"Greg" Gregory and his wife, Virginia, known as "Ginny," sleep in the master bedroom. It is an unusually large room over the unusually large den that has the reputation of being the center of most of the unconventional activity. In the middle of a cold November night in 1966, Greg was awakened by a ghastly moaning. He told me, "I listened to it for perhaps a minute. It seemed to be right in my bedroom, so I got up as quietly as I possibly could and moved toward the window away from the side of the bed to see if I could pinpoint the location of the sound. I finally walked toward the dresser so that the moaning was between me and the bed. This was approximately the last time I heard it because I then advanced very quickly to the spot where it came from and it stopped. When I turned on the light there was not a thing of any unusual nature to be seen in the room."

Greg's son Tucker and a friend who was visiting him heard the moaning from the room next door, which will be known for the rest of this narrative as "Kendall's room." Parham, another son, was awakened in his room at the far end of the hall. Oddly enough, Ginny was not aroused by the moan. Since her invisible houseguests do not favor one member of the family over another, however, she was treated to an ample sample on another occasion.

As is the custom of many persons who live in haunted abodes, Mrs. Gregory makes it a point to write down everything, so that there will be no confusion later about what actually occurred. She was sitting at the desk in her bedroom about seven o'clock one evening typing an account of the latest happening. She leaned back in her chair, relaxing a bit as she attempted to decide how to describe the moan that had been reported to her by her husband.

"I wonder just what kind of a moan it was," she thought, conjecturing about how to word her statement. At that moment what must have been the identical reverberation roared from the center of the bedroom. Ginny knew how to describe it then. It was "an indescribable, bubbling moan, a horrible, hideous sound as if someone were in unbearable agony. It lasted about fifteen seconds." It went on long enough that she had time to think, "This is impossible!"

After it ceased Ginny's first reaction was, "Somebody is playing a trick!" This was because it was the kind of noise someone would make if he were attempting to sound like a terrifying haunt. She rushed downstairs, but discovered that she was the only person there. Her husband was at a medical meeting; the smaller children were in the bathtub; and Ricky was studying in his room. Ginny even walked outside the house to see if the noise might have been made by a dog. "Then," she says, "I went into the kitchen and drank a glass of milk to try to calm my nerves.

"As I returned across the living room, in the far end toward the den I saw a very round, white, clear flash of light. The lamps were on in the other end of the long room, but the place where I saw the light was rather dimly illuminated. The flash was like the light that would come from a camera flash bulb, but small, round, and bright. It was followed by a 'flick' sound like the one that occurs when lightning strikes close to your house. The weather was quite calm, however."

Mrs. Gregory was so completely unnerved that night that she had to talk to someone, so she used the extension in her bedroom and phoned a friend. But while they were talking she began to hear footsteps on the upstairs porch. This is a long sleeping porch, the length of three bedrooms, and it has been glassed in. All the children's bedrooms open onto it, and the stairs come up to it from the living room. Ginny knew no one in heavy shoes should be out there at that time of night, so she hurriedly ended her phone conversation and rushed out the door. Because ghostly footsteps had been heard out there before, she was not surprised when she found the sleeping porch empty. In fact, she was rather relieved that it was not some human stranger, gun in hand. A ghost is probably preferable to a burglar. To some people, at least.

This charming and intelligent family who lives with haunts and takes them in stride—albeit with an occasional glass of milk for consolation—first came to my attention while I was visiting the Bradleys in Denver, Colorado. Dr. and Mrs. Robert A.

Bradley live in a haunted Tudor mansion called Bradmar, which is discussed in the last chapter of this book. *Medical Opinion and Review* for April 1969 carried Dr. Bradley's article about his hobby—psychical research—and it mentioned the ghost house in which he lives. While I was there Bob Bradley received a letter from Mrs. Kendall Gregory of Gulfport, Mississippi, stating that she and her husband, also a doctor, were delighted to learn that they could share their spectacular spectral problems with someone of similar medical interests and training. When the letter began to enumerate some of the apparitions and other phenomena the Gregorys had experienced, Bob handed it to me.

"This is a case for you," he said. He was right. We phoned Gulfport immediately and made arrangements for me to go there before I returned home.

It was spring along Mississippi's magical Gulf Coast when I was there, and the azaleas and wisteria were wild with it. Back of the haunted house is a trellis that leads from the porch several hundred feet down toward a nearby bayou. The trellis was completely covered with masses of pale purple clusters of wisteria that were so gorgeous to look at I could hardly make myself stay inside with the ghosts.

The dwelling itself is large, somewhat barnlike, somewhat dormitorylike, and about to fall apart, if it has not done so by the time this is published. The doctor has deliberately made no repairs lately because the place is so dilapidated it is not worth fixing up. And plans are under way for a new home to be built on the five and a half acres of beautifully treed and flowered slopes leading down to the bayou. After that, the old building will be destroyed. It is not likely that permission would have been granted for their story to be printed had the Gregorys not felt sure that the whereabouts of their haunting would probably be a thing of the past by the time this book is out.

Big and bulky as it is, the house still has a certain carefree, slapdash charm, as does any home that is the nesting place for a bunch of happy youngsters.

This is one of those Yours, Mine, and Ours families. Both Ginny and Greg had children by previous marriages, and now they have some together. Grier, a twenty-four-year-old Gulfport attorney, is Greg's oldest son. His other son, Tucker, now lives in Pennsylvania. Parham Bridges, a twenty-year-old recently stationed at Lackland Air Force Base, and Ricky Bridges, age eighteen, are Ginny's. The Ours generation are Kendall, Jr., who is fourteen; eleven-year-old Virginia, known as "Sister"; and John, only eighteen months old.

Although they had heard that the house had a reputation for being haunted, Dr. and Mrs. Gregory moved in anyway in September 1957. They did not believe in any such foolishness as ghosts. Even when Kendall, from the time he was about four or five, began to complain that something kept coming out of his closet and walking around his bed at night, he was not taken seriously.

The husky teenager told me that he remembered these experiences very clearly, even now. He said, "I woke up one night when I was about five and the closet door of my room was moving back and forth. I didn't think much about it and went back to sleep. Later I woke up again and there was something staring at me in the face. It was leaning over with its face close to mine. It looked like a boy, but I couldn't see it clearly."

"Did you say anything to it?" I asked.

"No. I jumped up and turned on the light and it disappeared. And a few nights later something came out of the closet again that was like a fluorescent color."

"Did you suspect it might be a ghost?"

"I didn't know anything about ghosts. Nobody ever talked about such things around our house . . . then."

Ginny said, "We began to think Kendall had a bogie-man complex. Finally when he started refusing to go to bed without the light on we moved him out of that room."

Sister had the same sort of problem with her parents. They did not believe her when she first told them about her funny experiences. It was only when the older folks began to see similar things that she was taken seriously. The quiet little tomboy told me she was about six the first time she saw it.

"Did you think it was a ghost?" I asked her.

"I didn't think about ghosts at all in connection with it," she replied. "No one had told me our house was haunted."

It was when she was sleeping in Kendall's room one night that the closet door opened and a light came out of it.

"I didn't know what it was, so I leaned up. Then I sat up and watched it," Sister said.

"I don't know why you didn't suspect it might be Tinker Bell," I remarked; but if Sister knew what I was talking about she gave no sign. She said the light opened the hall door and went outside. "I kicked Kendall and woke him up and asked him if he had a flashlight in the room.

"Kendall said, 'No,' but he sat up in bed. He wondered why I woke him in the middle of the night to ask him such a silly thing. He said I must be crazy. In the morning I told Mama about it. She didn't really believe me."

By the time Sister had her next big experience everyone was almost ready to take her account at face value. Her room with its little old-fashioned four-poster bed is in the middle between the two boys' rooms, and as long as she slept there nothing ever frightened or disturbed her. But sometimes when there was company or some special event she slept in Kendall's room, and then things happened.

She was in the bunk bed in Kendall's room when, she says, "I woke up about two in the morning and the closet door opened and it came out. It wasn't like fire, but looked like the heat waves over a fire. You know, what comes out of the fire in the fireplace . . . but glowing! It was exactly like that. I couldn't get the covers over my head like I usually do at night when I'm scared. I was struggling and trying to get under the covers but I couldn't and finally it went through my feet and I could feel this cold chill coming up my legs. It came around, like through me. I had my eyes shut. All of a sudden it got real dark, then it got light again."

"Now, wait a minute," I interrupted, trying to get the picture clear in my mind. "Where was this Thing?"

"It was bending over me. Standing right beside me inside against the wall, where there really isn't any room for anybody to stand. It leaned over. I was sort of shivering. It got up and walked through me again and went out. It was getting ready to open up the door when I fell asleep."

"You *what*? How could you possibly go to sleep at a time like that?"

"I don't know how I did it but I did it."

Ginny said, "I was impressed with her description of the glowing entity because it was so unusual that I thought she must actually have seen something. But it was not until the fall of 1963, when Grier came home one weekend from college at Ole Miss, that we really began to face the fact that the house might be haunted after all."

Grier's first experience can hardly be counted, because admittedly he and two college friends who accompanied him home had been out on the town and were boiled. They came in late and went to bed in the room only recently vacated by Kendall and the bogie man. Grier and Harvey got into the big double bed, but the boy who was supposed to sleep in the single bunk never made it.

"He was rather intoxicated," Grier said. "Actually, he was out cold on the floor with his head in the fireplace."

"In the fireplace?" I asked, startled.

"Oh, that was all right, there was no fire. Anyway, his head was in a wastebasket, as I recall." The young attorney grinned. "We tried to get him to bed but couldn't so we went ahead and turned out the light. Almost immediately the closet door opened and we could hear footsteps walking around the bed. We presumed it was our passed-out pal, trying to find the bathroom. Then Harvey saw a hand go past the window and hollered about it, so we turned on the light. Our companion was still stretched out on the floor. That is all that happened. I didn't see anything, but I heard footsteps. We suspected burglars, and with all that alcoholic energy we jumped out of bed and began to search the house over, even up to the third floor. But we didn't find anything."

Grier said that it was not until about two years later that he had his first genuine experience when he was sure he was not in a suggestible condition. I must say that when one is given lists of such goings-on about a house, it is easy to suspect that perhaps someone might be making things up for your benefit. Yet when you realize the integrity of the members of this family—a reputable physician, a busy lawyer, children with dignity and good manners, and a mother who keeps a home running efficiently for anywhere from five to nine people at a time, plus numerous friends who drop in casually—you know that it must be the dwelling place that is offbeat and not the people in it. None of them ever argues or expostulates about his beliefs. Each records the simple stories of what happened, just as one might describe a shopping expedition or a trip to the movies. All are sure that what they are telling is difficult for others to believe, but it has become a part of their lives and they have learned to accept it. They are still amazed from time to time at what happens, but they are used to it by now. When someone else remonstrates with them about their tales, they understand perfectly, for only a few years ago they would have reacted the same way in similar circumstances.

The simple account given by Grier is that the air conditioner in his bedroom cut out one night during the summer of 1965 and it was so hot that he decided to sleep in the den, where the cooling system was working. He slipped downstairs quietly so as not to disturb the others. Then, he says, "About four-thirty in the morning I was awakened by the door of the den opening and shutting. I looked over and a child was standing there, a boy. I glanced at the luminous dial of my wrist watch, wondering what my little brother was doing up. But then I thought, 'Why is he in the den? No one knows I'm down here.' So I looked back at the figure, and I could see the paneling of the door through it.

"Realizing this was some sort of apparition, I watched it carefully as it started moving in slow motion across the room. It was as if you ran a movie camera very slowly so that one frame turned every three seconds in sequencelike flashes. As the figure moved it became taller and less distinct and when it got to the corner of the den near the bookcase it disappeared. It was very light and sort of smoky, and had made the room luminescent; but when it left, everything became dark again. I stood up and turned on the pole light by the couch, then walked over and lit another pole light by the bookcase into which the figure had gone. I went back and sat down and thought about it for a few minutes; then I turned off the light by the couch and lay there a while longer before going to sleep. It started to rain outside, a really heavy summer shower.

"The next morning when I awoke I thought at first I'd had a strange dream. Well, I really knew I had been wide awake when it happened, but I tried to tell myself it was a dream. Then I noticed that the light was on across the room. Also, when I looked outside I saw that it had rained hard during the night."

The young attorney saw another apparition very briefly on the upstairs porch at about two-thirty in the afternoon of a summer's day; he has heard music and footsteps when he was in the house alone; and he had a fantastic experience in the den one night with two college girls.

Perhaps I'd better leave it there. What you think happened might be more fun than what did. However, the events were hardly prosaic. For the record, on the night of September 23, 1967, two visiting college girls named Barbara and Constance and Grier Gregory spent the night sitting up in the den to see if they could find any ghosts. They convened their meeting at 11:45 and adjourned at 5:00 A.M. if not wiser, certainly more confused. Grier has attempted to recall the events as nearly chronologically as he could, and here they are:

"Barbara and Connie began to hear singing and the sounds of a party, as if it were going on at a slight distance. There was music, talking, and laughter. Between one and two o'clock I started to hear the same sort of thing myself. We compared notes orally and agreed on several points. The sounds seemed to come from the general direction of the northeast corner of the room. They were sometimes distinct but more generally quite indistinct. At one point the three of us remarked that the sound of one man laughing loudly (almost a belly laugh) was particularly clear. Throughout we could hear the sound of a record playing a tinny old-fashioned tune, with the voice of a jazz or blues singer of about the 1920's period. Repeatedly, the record would seem to catch or get stuck when the singer hit a particular high note. The words of the song were indistinct, but Connie said that she could make out the beat or rhythm. This particular aspect lasted, on and off, for about one hour and stopped entirely about two o'clock.

"During the next hour and a half nothing whatsoever occurred. We got up from the couch in the southwest corner of the room where we had been sitting, went to the kitchen for coffee, and then returned and turned off the light again and waited for something to happen. We eventually grew quite impatient and orally demanded that the activity start."

According to Grier, about 3:30 Barbara cried, "Look at the light on the electric coffeepot!" It was moving up and down with a wobbling motion. Then it moved in a different direction. They began to tell it which way to go and it would follow their advice. For some time it moved in whatever direction they commanded it to move.

Then there was a period of time when figures became visible. Grier says, "I saw faces and figures around the light. Most were unremarkable and did not last for more than a few seconds. The figures seemed to be peering intently at the light and were confused, or rather bemused, by it. The figures and faces were solid in appearance, and they were in color. One was that of a man wearing a long white robe. Another was a man with a clean-cut profile wearing a striped shirt. At various times after that indistinct figures could be discerned moving about the room. Some were outlines, others were more like outlines filled with a smoky substance. One figure seemed to be sitting in a chair near the card table staring toward the fireplace. Another leaned against the card table and stared at us. Some of these various entities were visible for seconds only; others for considerable periods of time.

"At one point a figure of a man came over and sat down on the top of the coffee table in front of the couch on which I was sitting. It was perhaps 4:00 A.M. and I was brave by then, so I said to him, 'Can you touch me?' He reached out his hand but he was unable to reach me. I put out my hand to touch him but it was as if there were a wall between us; we couldn't touch. He did not seem alarmed or surprised by this fact.

"After a time we turned on the light again and smoked cigarettes while Connie went to the kitchen for some water. As Connie returned Barbara and I could clearly see a man following her. He was in formal dress, wearing a black coat, black trousers, and black tie, and his white shirt gleamed. He was fairly tall, and he followed her all the way back to the den. Then he stood and leaned against the door. Both Barb and I saw this clearly, but he was back of Connie all the while.

"Next we saw the figure of a little girl appear to walk through the door. She was quite distinct, a sort of Shirley Temple doll of a little girl with a full, frilly skirt, a sash, and lots of curls.

"Nothing much happened after that, and so pretty soon we decided to quit and go to bed. I left the girls and went upstairs. They slept in the den, but reported no further incidents."

Barbara's written account of the night is very similar to Grier's, and she also remarked about Connie's statements and reactions to various events. Connie's account, however, was not recorded until considerably later, and by then she had apparently had second thoughts. She stated that she was sure that the singing and music she heard had been caused by the droning of the air conditioner. According to the other two, the air conditioner was not on that night. Connie's remembrance of what she saw that most impressed her was of "Tiny pinpoint dots of light all over the room. It was rather like the particles of dust that you can see in a shaft of sunlight through a window. There were thousands of these little dots of light and they were in motion—probably dust particles being stirred up by the air conditioner and reflecting whatever light was present though too dim for us to perceive. I could stare at these dots and become hypnotized by them as one is hynotized by the falling snow when looking through the windshield of a moving car. . . . I continued to see them all night."

Grier and Barbara stoutly maintain that the air conditioner was not on at all during the entire night. It was late September and not hot enough to need it; and, anyway, they are sure that had it been on they would have questioned the music too, and wondered if it might not have been caused by the droning sound of the cooling system. As far as Grier and Barbara are concerned, imaginary air conditioners are no better than ghosts. They rather suspect that Connie, who had enthusiastically endorsed their comments and added observations of her own as to what she was seeing during the evening, had now rationalized the night's events into the type of prosaic explanation that she could live with. Or had the two of *them* unconsciously fabricated the figures they saw and the music they heard? In any other set of circumstances, such an argument might rationally be used. In *that* house, who knows?

An interesting confirmation of Grier's and Barbara's account occurred in July 1969, when a group of four persons the family knew well asked to spend the night in the haunted den.

Ginny assures me that there was no way any of these people could have been prepared by anything they might have heard that would have led them to expect a similar experience to Grier's. The youth had been especially careful not to speak of what happened, and the two girls with him were from out of town.

Ginny says, "These two couples who spent the night were extremely level-headed, cultured people. They came out of their experience in the den absolutely stunned by what they had heard."

What was it that had upset them so? The same sort of curious noises that had been described by Grier and Barbara. They had all heard the sounds of a riotous cocktail party going on there in the dark room.

Roderick Rhodes Bridges, the engaging eighteen-year-old known as Ricky, added another new dimension to the discussion with his account of his experiences. He said that when he was playing football in the ninth grade he came home late and tired one evening and dropped down on his bed with his clothes on and fell asleep. He woke up later to see the chest of drawers, which is directly in front of his bed, vibrating back and forth with abrupt, brisk movements, just as if somebody had hold of the top of it and was shaking it as a dog shakes a rag. "It did it for just a couple of minutes and then it stopped," Ricky said.

"Another night I was asleep and I don't know why I woke up but all of a sudden I just woke up and I looked at my dresser and the top drawer came out and then went back in again. Then the second drawer came out and went back in, and then all the way down, each drawer in turn came out and went back in. It was as if some invisible person were going through the drawers one at a time. I didn't know what to do, so I just turned over and went back to sleep."

I wondered if Ricky might not have dreamed the things he thought he saw. "Did you get up and move around or do anything so that you could be sure you weren't dreaming?" I asked him.

"No, I didn't get up. I went back to sleep," he answered. "The times that I've been awakened and seen things like that I just went back to sleep, but I was sure I had been awake. When I have a dream I can't remember it clearly; but when something like this happens I remember every bit of it the next morning or when I tell somebody about it. I don't necessarily have to get up and move around to know I'm awake."

Ricky went on with his narrative: "Then I was sleeping in Kendall's room one night when I was about fifteen or sixteen and I was in the little bed on the far side of the room. Pat Spear was spending the night with me and he was sleeping in the big bed. I don't know why I woke up then either, but I did. And I saw a figure floating near the ceiling. I didn't really know what it was, but it looked like gas fumes or heat coming off the road or something, yet it was in the form of like maybe a woman in a gown floating up there. I rubbed my eyes and looked again and it was still there. The figure was darker than the darkness of the room, but it was easy to see because the room wasn't all that dark. The porch light that stays on all night was showing in through the windows."

Ricky said that he usually does not go to bed until eleven-thirty or twelve because he stays up and studies, but nothing ever happens until he turns off the light. Then, he said, "When I am lying in my bed I can hear the floors creak and hear him walking around the room. When I turn the lights on he quits."

"Don't you think those boards might creak naturally?" I asked.

"No, ma'am, they creak under weight. When the house settles, or when it is windy, the walls creak, but the floors do not. Anyway, if it were merely the house settling, why would the sound stop the minute I turn on the light? It's the same way with the footsteps that we all hear sometimes running up and down the stairs. You hear them when you are in your room, but if you walk out and look at the stairs you can't hear the sound any more. But as soon as you go back into your room they start up again."

Ricky paused, trying to recall more personal accounts to tell me. He could think of none. "It's been a long time since I've heard anything," he said, "but it used to happen real often."

"Has anyone else been aware of recent activity?" I asked him.

"Parham said just before he left for Lackland, 'The ghost was cutting up again last night.' He had heard footsteps. And Grier has heard it recently, too," he answered. His statement was corroborated by his mother. Also, Ginny said, it was only about six or seven months ago that she saw a man in her bedroom.

"I awakened," she said. "I don't know what time it was, but it was dark, and there was the figure of a man standing at the foot of the bed. He was somehow in the air, I guess, because he seemed raised up some two feet off the floor. He was in the center of the footboard, behind it but with just his feet below it. I thought for a second it was Greg, because he was a big man. I could not see his face clearly, but I could see everything else. He had on a brown plaid sport coat and dark brown trousers and a white shirt. The way he stood and looked at me was very peculiar. He had his chin in the palm of his right hand and his left hand under his right elbow and he was staring at me. He didn't move, but I was very aware of being watched. I turned my face away and closed my eyes for a second, then looked back and he was still there. I did it again and when I looked back I could see just his silhouette. Then he was gone."

What Mrs. Gregory particularly did not understand about this specter was that he did not have any facial features. "Is that unusual?" she asked me.

In all my experience as a spook sleuth I have learned only one consistent thing about ghosts—their inconsistency. I replied, "It is hard to say what is usual and what is unusual about these things. It seems to me that anything goes as far as ghosts are concerned."

That bed that the Gregorys sleep in is a rare and valuable Mallard half-tester canopy bed made in New Orleans probably in the first part of the nineteenth century. It has a massive headboard carved in a shell motif that stands nine or ten feet high on big mahogany legs. The posts at the foot of the bed are nine feet tall. They have sections that can be moved so that women in the old days could throw their corset strings over them and use the leverage of the post to pull the strings tight to achieve a tiny waist, à la Scarlett O'Hara.

One night in this bed Ginny had an uneasy sensation that kept her from sleeping. She was lying there rigid when all of a sudden there was a sharp sound like somebody with long fingernails clicking them against the headboard. It woke Greg, who got up, turned on the lights, and looked under the bed. Finding nothing suspicious, he went back to sleep. Ginny still had a feeling of apprehension. She says, "I lay there and thought, 'What am I going to do if this thing starts banging on the headboard of the bed?' About thirty or forty-five minutes later I found out. There was this resounding crash, as if somebody had taken the flat of his hand and slapped the headboard. It was the loudest thing I ever heard. I screamed! Greg got up and searched around, but there was nothing that had caused it. Later we went through all the experiments, pounding on the floor and on the wall and the headboard to see if we could recreate the sound. But we could not."

Greg said about this incident, "I went out on the screened-in porch to see if anything could be blowing, the screens or cabinet doors. I even went down into the den and took a pool cue and rapped against the floor to see if I could reproduce the sound. But there was nothing we could find that even came close to the sound because it seemed to come directly from the headboard of the bed."

It would appear that the ghost had read Ginny's mind and knew she was frightened of the very phenomenon it then managed to produce. There was another incident that also revealed her mental rapport with the invisible entities that were intruding themselves into her home. One evening Dr. Gregory came home from his office with a pamphlet which described the treatment for a particularly unusual disease. He had encountered such a case among his patients that day and wanted to study up on it. He left the pamphlet on the bedside table after he had read it, and he went to sleep.

As she lay beside him in the bed Ginny's mind wandered aim-
lessly before she slept. She happened to think about a particular
pet recipe of hers that had been lost at the time she moved into
the ghost house about fourteen years before. She says, "I was
thinking what a shame it was that I had lost the recipe because
when we get our new house I will be able to entertain large
groups again, and this was a wonderful casserole for crowds. I
hadn't seen it since we moved. It had just disappeared.

"The next morning we got up and had breakfast and then
Greg went upstairs to pick up the pamphlet and take it to the
office with him. He couldn't find it and called for me. I had not
touched it, but it certainly wasn't where he had left it, so I
helped him search. We looked everywhere for it, and it was just
nowhere to be found. With its bright orange cover, it would not
be easy to lose—but lost it obviously was.

"Greg left for the office and soon I went to the grocery store.
When I returned I sat down and started thinking about the pamphlet. I got some kind of impression about it—I guess you would
call it 'psychic,' wouldn't you? I thought, 'If the spook has taken
Greg's pamphlet, he has carried it to the third floor and if I go
up there I'll find it.'

"I went upstairs and entered the big room over our bedroom.
Then I walked on through it and into the little storeroom back of
it. The first thing I saw on the floor was my lost recipe! It is in a
little booklet that was lying in the center of the floor. No, indeed,"
she answered an unasked question, "it had not been there the last
time I was in that little room, and it couldn't have fallen off something and landed where it was. It was right out in the center of
the bare floor. I picked it up and took it downstairs.

"Greg came home for lunch and looked all over the bedroom
again for his pamphlet. He still could not find it. Shortly after he
returned to the office I was watching one of the television soap
operas I am hooked on and right in the middle of it, it suddenly
occurred to me, 'If the purpose of all this was for me to find the
recipe, I have found it. So the pamphlet should be back where it

was.' I walked over to the bedside table and it was there! We could never have missed that brilliant orange cover when we looked so carefully before, if it had been there then."

Another of Ginny's strange psychic perceptions helped her to learn the identity of the principal haunt in her house. Ginny may be the catalyst here—the mediumistic person whose abilities allow the ghosts to manifest. There have been frequent reports of activity when she was not at home, however, so I cannot be too dogmatic in my statement. But some of her presentiments seem to have had more behind them than the mere Fickle Finger of Fate.

Apparitions of two men have been described on several occasions, but it is the young boy who appears most often. Who is this child? Ginny conjectured that he might be the fourteen-year-old son of the previous owner of the house, who was killed in a tractor accident on the property. She thinks she was led in a roundabout way to receive verification of this. It all started with fires.

In the summer of 1963 a maid found a candle burning on top of a cabinet in the kitchen. It was a short, chunky, red candle of a size and shape and color that was not likely to have been brought into the house by any member of the family; and all disclaimed having ever seen it before. Later in the summer Ginny found a similar red candle burning behind closed doors in the cabinet under the kitchen sink. No connection with ghosts was suggested at this time, because, as has already been noted, there was almost no suspicion of them that early.

Then one afternoon in October, Parham came home after school, went upstairs, and walked into his room. Nobody else was upstairs. As he opened the door, the lining of a blue school jacket lying on the foot of his bed burst into flames. He put the fire out and took the jacket downstairs to show his mother. There was a line six or seven inches long of holes ranging in size from a dime to a quarter that had been burned across the back.

Ginny said, "The burned places were still smoldering when I saw them. I don't know why, but at that moment I got it into my head for some strange reason that we should try to get in touch with the family of the boy who was killed here. I started immediately making an effort to locate some of them. I discovered that there was only one person on the Coast related to him—an aunt—and when I finally found her in the phone book through the name of the company she and her husband operated, it turned out that they were in the *fire protection* business! Maybe you would call that coincidence, but I don't. I think the fires were deliberately set to be the cause of our getting in touch with the boy's family. The aunt came out for a visit with us, and later when the boy's mother returned to Gulfport I met her and talked with her." All this ultimately helped to identify the young ghost; but the Gregorys do not want his name mentioned because they are sure his mother would not like publicly to have her son identified as an "earthbound" spirit who has been haunting a house.

The way the identification came about is as mixed-up and kinky as everything else involving ghosts usually is: Ann Bell Adam and her husband, Robert Adam, both since deceased (their story will be told in a later chapter), were friends of Ginny's and Greg's. Fortunately for our records they left affidavits, dated in October 1965, about the apparition Ann saw in the Gregory house.

One day in the fall of 1963 Ann was visiting Ginny while Dr. Gregory was out of town. The telephone rang and it was a long-distance call from Greg, so Ann politely walked out into the kitchen so as not to overhear Ginny's conversation. There she surprised a young boy listening in on the extension in the kitchen. Ann scolded him severely, telling him he should know better than to eavesdrop and to put the phone down immediately. The boy stared at Ann in a most unconcerned manner, obeyed her without a word, and turned and walked out the back door. After a brief moment, in which Ann realized that she did not know that boy, she followed him out the door. He was gone, although there was no place he could have hidden in such a short time . . . if he had been made of flesh and blood.

When Ginny joined her friend, Ann said, "I think I've just seen your ghost!" The two women looked all over the yard for him, but he was gone, completely!

Having so recently been in touch with the family of the boy who formerly lived in the house, Ginny thought perhaps she could procure a picture of him, and she did. Then she called Ann and asked her to come over to see a picture that she suspected might be the telephone boy. Ann told her husband before she left home that even if the picture was of the same boy she would not admit it to Ginny for fear it would frighten her. Also, since the boy's mother had moved back to town, Ann did not want to upset her by having her learn that her dead son was haunting a house.

The affidavit tells Ann's story of that day: "When I arrived at Mrs. Gregory's house a little later she showed me a small, clear picture of the type taken at schools for the children's class pictures depicting the head and shoulders of a young boy. I was very certain and I am still convinced that it was the same boy I had seen that afternoon; however, I told Mrs. Gregory that I couldn't be sure one way or the other. Mrs. Gregory then told me that the picture was of the boy who had formerly lived in that house and had been killed there. On my arrival home I told my husband what had happened and that I identified it as the same boy."

The affidavit signed by Robert B. Adam testified to the same thing, that his wife had told him that the picture was of the boy she saw, even though she had not admitted it to Mrs. Gregory.

Ann Adam later did tell Ginny that she had identified the boy in the picture as the ghost; and that was when the women rushed to the lawyer to have the affidavits drawn up.

Another interesting event that happened that same fall was the blood on the windows. Ginny recalls the exact date of that one without having to look in her records. It was on November 17, 1963, that Parham and Ricky, who had slept in the north bedroom, came running in to her at breakfast saying there was blood all over their windows. Ginny says, "We went upstairs and found blood smeared in circles on two windows and splashed on the draperies. I scraped it off with a razor blade and Greg took it to the lab and it was human blood, RH-positive. I do not see how any of the children could have bled enough to have caused all that amount of it without my knowing about it. They all insisted they did not. Kendall might have had a nosebleed, but he was little and I would have known. I just don't think it happened normally. Perhaps it was a prediction of the Kennedy assassination that occurred just a few days later."

In a house full of children it is natural to look to them for the answer to any seeming prank, before supernormal explanations are suspected. In fact, the first day I was there, before I had met all the children who were at home, I asked Dr. and Mrs. Gregory just how positive they were that their young fry had not invented the stories they had been telling me. "Are any of your children the type who might be inclined to play pranks and make up things of this sort?" I asked.

Ginny answered, "I don't think so about anything like this. Do you, Greg?"

Her husband replied, "We wondered about it at the beginning. In fact, we even talked to them about it, implying that we suspected this was not a real haunting. But we never elicited anything from any of them that was in the least suspicious."

"Anyway," pointed out his wife, "it isn't always the children who are involved, as you have seen. We personally have experienced so much, and when something happens to us later that is somewhat similar to what they have described earlier—then we naturally realize that they must have been telling the truth. Also, the servants have seen the ghosts, and lots of outsiders have had queer experiences here. Several young psychologists have

spent the night in the den from time to time. It is amusing how
they reacted to their experiences. Two of them heard the sound
of something being dragged across the floor. One said to the
other, 'Don't be silly. That's no ghost. That's a raccoon or a 'possum that's gotten up in the rafters of the basement and is playing
around.' He was completely satisfied with that answer; but it was
not very scientific, because there is no basement under the den
and it has a concrete floor. He could have discovered this by a
small amount of investigation."

"Then," recalled Dr. Gregory, "there was the group that said
they had no results at all. They spent the night there and said
nothing happened. Then they added that the ticking of the
grandfather clock had been so loud all night they couldn't have
heard anything else anyway. They forgot to look around to see
that there was no grandfather clock in the room, nor any other
clock. Nor do we have one outside the den that can be heard
there."

Ginny added, "People have heard invisible candelabra tinkling
in there, too, when the wind blew the crystal prisms together.
But there once were candelabra, and also a large clock, on the
mantelpiece of the den. That was at the time of the original owners, the Stewarts. I have talked to people who used to visit them
here then."

Among other outsiders who have had experiences in the house
they cannot account for is a young attorney, whose fiancée told
me this story about his experience. They were invited to the
Gregorys' for dinner one evening in the summer of 1968, and
after dinner they all sat in the living room and talked. This long
room has a fireplace at each end. Grouped around each is an
arrangement of chairs, couches, tables, and lamps. The "sitting
room" most popular with the family is the end close to the dining
room, and the young couple (Bill and Jane, we'll call them) sat
on the couch there. It was a warm evening but Bill complained
of feeling a chill and said the hair of his neck was standing up.
One might suspect that he was reacting as he thought proper for

a visit to a haunted house, except that he was no stranger there.

All during the evening Bill kept hearing a sound coming from the far end of the living room. It was like growling, as if made by some invisible dog hiding behind the mirror over the fireplace —the one that backs against the den.

Now, on the morning of that day, Chester, a young dog owned by the family, had been run over and killed. Thor, the large, black German Shepherd dog with the sweetest disposition any police dog ever had, was allowed in the house that night because he was mourning Chester's death so miserably. But Thor never seemed to hear the growling that so disturbed Bill. Every once in a while all evening the lawyer would say, "There it is again! Don't you hear it?" When no one else did, Bill was completely stumped.

Several of the servants who have worked for the Gregorys over the years have had odd experiences. I talked to Mrs. Myrtis Peters, a Negro woman of forty-nine, who had several accounts for the record. As is usual in the case of such reminiscences, the specific years are rather vague, but the events themselves are seared in the mind. Myrtis told me that about ten in the morning of an early fall day when the children were in school and Mrs. Gregory had gone out, she saw a tall, bareheaded man in gray trousers and a dark gray sweater go into the den.

"I did not know it was a ghost then," she said. "I just thought it was one of the boys who come in here sometimes, but I didn't recognize him. When he didn't come out of the den I got my sister-in-law, Eva Peters, who was also working here then, and we went in and looked for him. There was no one there."

On another occasion Myrtis Peters was in the kitchen preparing breakfast. She noticed out of the corner of her eye that someone in a dark suit and white shirt was standing by the table reading the paper. A little later Mrs. Gregory came in and asked her for the morning paper. Mrs. Peters said, "Dr. Gregory got it."

"No," said Ginny, "Dr. Gregory has not come down yet." And sure enough, there was the paper, still rolled up. Then when the

doctor came downstairs he wore his robe because it was Thursday, his day off. It was before eight o'clock, and the children
were not up yet."

Myrtis added, "We hear things, too. Once before Eva quit
working we were upstairs. There was nobody but us in the house.
And the cat. We had cats then. We heard such a loud crash
downstairs that we thought the cat had knocked over one of the
big lamps in the living room or something. We came rushing
down to look and nothing was broken anywhere. And the cat
was upstairs."

Eva Peters saw the boy early one cold winter morning. She arrived in her car and as she was parking it by the garage she saw
a youngster, maybe fourteen, walking under the trees looking up
into them. When Eva got out of her car and approached him, he
vanished. Another time Eva and Charles, a yard-and-houseman,
heard footsteps upstairs when they knew nobody was there.

Charley was once cleaning the living room when he saw a boy
coming around the curve of the driveway. He went to the front
door to let him in, but the boy went on by. Through the windows
Charley could see him walking past, so he hurried through to the
kitchen door and opened it, but nobody came. He got Eva and
they went outside and looked all around but there was no boy.

We have accounted for the phantom presence of the boy, as a
child who was killed on the property. What of the men who have
been seen as ghosts? Is there any known excuse for their presence? Historically, perhaps there is. The big house was originally
built in 1915 and various families have lived in it. Then, in 1941
it was leased to the Air Force to be used as a Non-Commissioned
Officers' Club during World War II. It was operated by a sergeant who lived there and was not averse to illegal activity. He
moved gambling equipment into the master bedroom. (Perhaps
the moaner is a former heavy loser at craps or roulette!) He also
kept a supply of women on the premises—for immoral purposes,
no doubt. As a result the place was closed by the government.

It is a known fact, Ginny says, that this sergeant returned

after the war and tore open a window seat on the third floor and dug out a hidden fortune in savings bonds which he declared to be his "cut." This man, who was short and dark and a typical gambler, has been dead for some years now. His description is similar to that of one of the ghosts seen several times.

A laundress named Susan saw someone who looked like him. Susan had been standing at the foot of the kitchen table folding the laundry when this man came out of the downstairs bathroom, which opens into the butler's pantry. He walked out through the open door and stared her square in the face, and it frightened her so that she could feel her hair "drawing up," as she put it. Susan described the man as about five feet seven inches tall, around forty years of age, with a sharp face. He wore a little white cap with a snap in the front, like those worn in the nineteen-thirties, and he had on black pants and a white shirt.

After this apparition had stared at Susan he walked through the door into the dining room, then across the end of the living room and up the stairs. The maid followed him and heard his footsteps as he climbed. But Mrs. Gregory was upstairs and she observed that no man came up. The two women looked in every room of the house for him, but he had disappeared.

Ginny told me, "I think there is no doubt that he was the sergeant in charge of the house when it was an NCO Club. We believe something terrible happened in the house then. The moaning and screaming we've heard may come from that time, and the sound of something heavy being dragged across the floor. Oddly enough, the mother of the boy—who lived here just before we moved in—said they had heard that sound. The only things she reported having heard were the footsteps and this dragging.

"Perhaps some of the grotesque things that happened then still remain captured in the atmosphere of the house," I suggested. "They may be memory images of some kind."

"I certainly hope we find out before the house is torn down just what caused all this," Ginny said. "Sometimes I nearly die of curiosity about it." Then she recalled something that had happened to Parham that seemed to fit into the picture she had just been discussing. "One night Parham went down to the kitchen about two-thirty to get something to eat so he could go back to sleep. He heard the sound of someone moaning in either the living room or the den and he could distinguish a woman's voice saying, 'Get out! Get out!' over and over again. Then he heard what he described as very forceful but not particularly loud screaming."

When Parham walked back through the living room he saw that the den was lighted up; but he did not avail himself of the opportunity to learn what was going on. Can we blame him? A year or so earlier Parham had another frightening experience. He had been a "slip boy" at a local bridge tournament in which his mother had been playing. She returned home when it was over; but the slip boys had to stay to gather up all the cards and put everything away, so Parham did not get home until midnight. Just after he had gone to bed a book fell off his desk. It would be interesting if he had thought to notice what the title of the volume was, but he did not. Then he heard his name called in a peculiarly childish voice. It sounded, he said, like a child calling through a length of pipe. He sat up in bed and saw in the light reflected from the porch a shadow move across the illuminated area of his room. Startled, he got up and walked around. Near the mantel he felt a particularly cold breeze. Even more disturbed by that, he jumped back into bed, and then he felt the cold in there as well. This is the event that impressed Parham most of anything in which he has been involved in the house, his mother told me.

What impresses *me* most is how all these young people accept the things that happen to them without running screaming into the night. The spunky kids have actually quelled ghostly activity on occasion. Sister was worried a lot by the sound of her metronome ticking, although it was not actually going. She told me, "I heard it at night. Then I heard it the next morning. For about two weeks I heard it and finally I said, 'Whoever you are, just stop that. I'm getting tired of it.' And it just quit and I never heard it again."

Another time, Ginny told me, "Parham got tired of some of the foolishness around there. He spoke to it and said, 'Either put up or shut up. Either produce or stop the racket,' and it stopped." Ginny glowed with motherly pride when she talked about her children. "Parham's not afraid of the devil," she added. We did not suspect the devil of any machinations in this house, however; but only an odd couple of older men and a young boy.

I was in Gulfport over April First and so we decided to hold an April Fool's Day séance. The Gregorys insisted that they did not want any kind of an exorcism ceremony performed that would run their ghosts off. They had got along with them this far; they figured to get along with them now until it was all over and the house destroyed. After all, there is nothing more exciting and entertaining than ghostly manifestations, after you have once learned to live with them. If a medium were to become entranced and any of the entities were to speak through her, it might have been possible to explain to them their situation and talk them out of continuing their haunting. This is not the strictly religious exorcism ceremony, but is a means frequently used to rid a house of ghosts.

We found ourselves unable to locate a medium, anyway; but we decided to go ahead with the séance, hoping that the natural psychic abilities of some of the group might provide whatever physical force was necessary to produce phenomena. Ginny invited twelve friends who are interested in psychical things. Also included was clinical psychologist Dr. James C. Crumbaugh, who does a lot of work in parapsychology, and Flint Liddon of Jackson, Mississippi, a friend of mine whom we also discovered to be a cousin of Ginny's.

For several hours we sat in a circle in the den in the dark—only the barest minimum of light was coming in through the windows from outside. We talked and enjoyed ourselves throughout the evening. There is one school of thought that insists that sé-ances must be held in absolute quiet. We were subscribing to the theories of the other school, which believes that happy and inter-ested conversation enlivens the physical conditions and makes it possible for spirits to use the power we thus generate to perform their manifestations.

With all our efforts, absolutely nothing supernormal occurred. In fact, we dispersed shortly after midnight convinced that the ghosts had played their April Fool joke on us by not appearing. The next day, however, as Ginny and I were discussing the pre-vious evening's washout, we began to realize that we had experi-enced a correspondence in our thinking that might be considered a bit phenomenal. Ginny and I had been sitting across from each other in the circle. In development classes those who sit opposite are known as "batteries." I do not know why it is true, but ex-perience has taught me that it is a fact that batteries frequently have the same or very similar thoughts while sitting quietly in the circle.

Now, we had not sat quietly, as I said. All during the evening we had talked freely about psychical phenomena. We had also discussed in detail the philosophy that arises among those who have seen indications of the valid existence of ghosts and believe that they occasionally bring evidence for the survival of the human soul after death. We did not at any time talk about the possible identity of the ghosts that haunted this house.

All during that evening, as we sat and talked, I had been con-stantly alert to answer the questions put to me. I was also ana-lyzing every sound I heard or movement made by members of the circle, in case any manifestations might be starting. I kept hoping, in a half-hearted sort of way, that one of those famous cold-blooded moans would come just back of my right ear in an area of the room where no human could have produced it. On top of all this I was making a vigorous effort to keep myself from getting sleepy or falling into any kind of trancelike state. My experience in Machias, Maine (to be reported later), had convinced me that I might be mediumistic if I allowed myself to be, and I had no desire to be taken over or influenced in any way by the Gregory ghosts.

With all this in my mind, it is obvious that I was not concentrating on the personalities of the spirits who might be around us. I wanted them to keep their distance, but also to produce genuine phenomena. That was more than enough to expect of them. I did not once think consciously of the boy ghost. Yet twice during the evening I had very poignant feelings for him. Once briefly I thought that a man dimly observable across the circle from me took on the appearance of a woman sitting there cuddling a boy in her lap. Then, right at the end of the evening I had a feeling of incredible yearning, a real sadness, and I knew it was for that child, invisibly in our presence.

At the same time Ginny was sitting opposite me in the dark—my battery—enduring a feeling of deep sorrow. In her mind the words kept repeating over and over again, "Poor little boy, poor little boy."

Why did he remain in the house? Was he clinging after death to his earthly surroundings because he enjoyed the pleasure of trying to attract the attention of the young people in the family? Or did he feel left out of things? Might he somehow be lost and in need of enlightenment and liberation? As Ginny and I realized that we had both reached out in our thoughts to this child, we began to suspect that we may have somehow got to him. Perhaps now he would understand, after all the discussion at that evening séance, that he does not have to remain there as an unseen presence, that he can move on to a fuller and more rewarding existence with enlightened spirits who are just waiting for his acquiescence to help him.

Perhaps somehow we had been able to set those young ghostly feet on a more constructive and rewarding path. We hoped so.

CHAPTER VI

┊┋┊┋┊┋┊┋

Ghosts in a
Governor's Mansion

HOW LONG CAN a house maintain a reputation for being haunted when all its ghosts are ancient and no one involved with it cares to see their tradition perpetuated? The home of the Governor of Delaware has such a problem. It is beautiful enough, and gracious enough, to maintain itself as a showplace on the strength of its charm and historical interest alone, and that is all that is expected of it. Still, the ghostly legends just will not get lost.

Stately Woodburn, a fine Middle Period Georgian house on King Street in Dover, is the first official governor's residence Delaware has ever owned. It was not until 1966 that the Delaware General Assembly appropriated funds for the purchase and restoration of an estate for this specific purpose. Former governors either lived in their own homes or rented houses.

The plot of ground on which the Executive Mansion stands was part of a tract of three thousand acres given by William Penn "at Dover this 7th of ye 3rd month 1683" to John Hillyard. John's great-grandson, Charles Hillyard, built the large brick house in 1790 on his farm, which was then about a mile out of town. He used exquisite taste in its construction, ending up with a house quite fit for a governor's social duties, with drawing, music, and dining rooms, wide hallways, and seven bedrooms. It has beautifully paneled walls, attractive fireplaces, big sunny windows, and a gloomy cellar for the ghosts.

The first colorful story to come down to us about the house involves this same Charles Hillyard, who, in a fit of passion, chased one of his sons, pistol in hand, and fired at him just as he ran through the front door. This is a Dutch door, a double one cut in two horizontally, and the son saved his life by slamming it behind him. The ball entered the door instead of the youth, and this is all we know about the incident. With that tantalizing brevity so many old documents have, which tells us only half a story, we have no details whatever as to what mischief the son had been up to that so infuriated his father. But that the incident actually happened is attested to by Judge George Purnell Fisher in a paper of the Historical Society of Delaware entitled "Recollections of Dover in 1824." Judge Fisher wrote, "When I lived in the house in 1878 there was a small piece of wood fitted into the bullet hole to hide it." Today all evidence of it has disappeared. But . . . could the irascible old Charles Hillyard, refusing to leave his lovely home, be one of the haunts? He sounds like good material for it.

It is to Judge Fisher that we also turn for the first genuine mention of a ghost at Woodburn. He reported that on one occasion Lorenzo Dow stopped at the estate for a visit with "leading Methodists" Dr. M. W. Bates and his wife, who lived there at the time. Fisher wrote that on coming downstairs for breakfast Mr. Dow passed on the stairway "a gentleman dressed in the fashion of the preceding generation with queued hair, knee breeches, ruffled bosom, etc. When Dow went into the breakfast room, on being asked to lead in family prayer, he suggested whether they had better not wait until their other guest, whom he met going upstairs, should come down. Mrs. Bates said there was no other guest in the house—only himself. This evoked from Dow a de-

scription of the gentleman whom he met on the stairs." Mrs.
Bates, it seems, made some quite evasive remarks in reply, and
they proceeded to prayer and then to breakfast. After the meal
was over, she quietly suggested to Lorenzo Dow that he should
not reveal the incident. This was because "his personal description of the mysterious guest pictured her father who had been
dead for quite a number of years." Judge Fisher somewhat causti-
cally comments that it was said "that Dow was never afterwards
entertained at the Bates House."

As this is written, the newly elected Governor of Delaware,
Russell Peterson, and his wife have not yet moved into Woodburn, it being in the process of undergoing its spring houseclean-
ing and the rearrangings and alterations usual at a time when
new incumbents arrive. Much had already been revealed about
the house and its haunts, however, in interviews with the previous occupants, Governor and Mrs. Charles L. Terry, Jr. They
were extremely gracious but slightly cagey when talking about
ghosts. Certainly they never saw any during the time they lived
at Woodburn . . . and yet . . . neither did they deny that they may
have been sensitive to certain nuances . . . an atmosphere . . .
vibrations.

I did not have the opportunity to talk to Mrs. Terry until after
she had moved out of Woodburn; but as she put it to me, "You
feel the presence of history in that house." She assured me she
knew nothing but happiness there. I accepted that, for the pleasure of living in a home of historical significance must be enormous.

Mrs. Terry had been equally charming, yet equally evasive
about the haunts with reporter Barbara Barnes of the Philadelphia *Sunday Bulletin Magazine* who had interviewed her for an
article entitled "The Governor and the Ghosts" in April 1966,
shortly after the State of Delaware acquired the house.

Barbara asked Mrs. Terry if there had been any real evidence
of ghosts since she had moved in.

"I couldn't be sure of that," Mrs. Terry replied gaily. "I am a light sleeper. Sometimes I hear footsteps on the stairs at night. But probably they are just the natural settling of an old house."*

One can understand that a governor's wife, or a former governor's wife, would not care to be put on the spot about whether or not the official residence is haunted. If she admitted she believed it, or related any personal experiences, some of her husband's constituents might have resented it. Yet if she said she did not believe in such things, or had no psychic experiences in the house, some others might think her insensitive. I believe Mrs. Terry handled her questioners very well when she made such observations as, "It's fun to live in a place that's distinguished enough to have legends. In England every house worth its history has a ghost or two." I mean, you can't beat that for tact and subtlety.

I loved Mrs. Terry anyway. She sounds when she talks exactly like the fabulous Mrs. Richard J. Hughes, wife of the ex-Governor of New Jersey, who is so delightful in her television appearances on the "Mike Douglas Show." Mrs. Terry is pretty, too—a dainty, slender woman with a warm smile, silver hair, blue eyes, and camellialike skin. She loves Woodburn, and it can easily be understood that she was eager to talk about the house itself and its beautiful antiques as well as its ghosts. It was she who assisted State Archivist Leon deValinger, Jr., in the search for furnishings for the 176-year-old house after it was purchased by the state for a governor's mansion. Furniture appropriate to the age in which it was built has been used throughout.

"We tried to find furniture made in Delaware, the Delmarva Peninsula, and nearby parts of Pennsylvania," Mrs. Terry said as she showed Barbara Barnes through the house. She pointed out a handsome Queen Anne highboy, a stately grandfather clock, a tea table and other eighteenth- and early-nineteenth-century pieces. The rugs are antique or semiantique Orientals which are compatible with the woodwork and furnishings of the

* Reprinted with permission from *The Sunday Bulletin Magazine*. Copyright 1966 Bulletin Co.

rooms. Miss Barnes noted that "the two restorers are especially proud of a collection of Staffordshire china made originally for Delaware's naval hero in the War of 1812, Commodore Thomas Macdonough. Pieces of it were found in many out-of-the-way places. Some of it was donated."

Mrs. Terry laughed when she showed the reviewer an antique decanter. "One of our legends concerns a decanter like this," she said. "A former owner of the house claimed he filled it every evening and by morning ghosts had consumed most of the wine."

As soon as the new governor's family is settled in Woodburn, it will be open to the public again, probably on Tuesday and Thursday afternoons. Many who visit it go in anticipation of seeing ghosts, because of their elusive fame. They usually ask first about the Dead Man's Tree, if they have not already identified it as they came in. Among the many old trees and specimen pieces of shrubbery on the spacious grounds of the Governor's House are ancient pines, crepe myrtles, and old English boxwood; and to the east of the house is a large boxwood maze in the formal garden. But the Dead Man's Tree is right in front of the house, so large that it looms through the many-paned front windows. It is a gnarled old poplar with eerie-looking apertures in its hollow trunk.

The most interesting story about the house involves this tree, but Leon deValinger assures me it is nothing but legend. The tale goes that in pre-Civil War days Woodburn was a station on the Underground Railway. A secret tunnel was supposed to lead from the great, dark cellar of this house to the nearby St. Jones River. (This is not a misprint. Since 1670 the river has been designated on documents as "St. Jones" although no one knows where the name came from or why it is spelled that way.) Runaway slaves were hidden in the cellar, according to an old *New York Times* clipping I have, until the time came that they were spirited away through the tunnel to a boat on the river, and ultimate safety. There is no evidence in the cellar today that a tunnel ever led into it. However, this report of the runaway slaves has been going around for many years, and *The New York Times* and I are stuck with it.

How did the ghost get hung up in the tree? The *Times* version is that one night Southern raiders came to the Underground Railway station and attempted to capture the slaves hidden there to sell them back to their owners. The occupant of Woodburn then, a Quaker named Daniel Cowgill, drove the raiders off. For some reason one of them did not retreat with the others, but hid out in the hollow of the big old tree. Somehow he accidentally slipped and got his head caught in a hole of the tree and hung there until he was dead, and good riddance. Children of the neighborhood are said still to insist that on a clear night you can see the dead man hanging in the tree.

Mrs. Terry said that as a Southerner she was brought up on ghost stories. The children would sit around the fire at night telling tales until they were scared to go to bed. She thinks she got so much of it then that she no longer has any fear. If she had seen any ghosts at Woodburn, though, she knows they would have been friendly. She loved the old house so much that she is sure anyone who haunted it would be nice.

Maybe the other historical ghost for whom there is little evidence but a lot of rumor—the one who glides about from time to time in Revolutionary War costume—is a pleasant one, along with Mrs. Bates's father. If there is any occasionally visible haunt hanging from that tree out front, however, I cannot credit him with being agreeable. He was a "bad guy" on earth and a bad guy he must still be until he learns the futility of frequenting the scene of his horrible death. Because of him and him alone I can understand the claim that after dark the children of Dover still run as they pass the King Street Governor's Mansion.

CHAPTER VII

Miami Poltergeist
Revisited

THE LAST CHAPTER of *Prominent American Ghosts,* dealing
with "Miami's Pertinacious Poltergeist," ended with the words
"To be continued" because it was obvious there would be more
to come in this curious case. I did not dream *how* much! Now
this book brings the story up to date, providing much additional
information in the strange saga of Julio Vasquez, a youth en-
chanted. If we knew who or what has put him under this spell,
perhaps we could do more to help him.

Poltergeists, those strange invisible forces reported throughout
history as causing dishes to fly, stones to rain from ceilings, bottles to pop their caps, and boxes to crash from shelves all apparently of their own volition, are accounted for in different ways
by different people. Psychokinesis, or the power of the human
mind over physical matter, is undoubtedly behind the activity,
and this force comes from the subconscious mind of one specific
individual. He is frequently, but not necessarily, a child in pu-
berty. It is natural that he is suspected of trickery and carefully
watched; it is important that witnesses attempt to be critical and
objective even when they are in the midst of tumultuous inexplic-

able action. It is seldom, however, that the besieged person is ever *proved* to be fraudulent, for many events occur that no child or even an intelligent adult would be capable of producing.

In my previous account of Julio and the poltergeist I indicated that many careful observers had investigated him. For twenty-two days in January and the first two days of February 1967, in Tropication Arts on N. E. 54th Street in Miami, which sells wholesale novelty items for ten-cent stores and gift shops, exciting activity occurred daily as hundreds of dishes, mugs, and boxes dashed themselves from shelves. In the warehouse while this was going on were policemen, researchers, newspaper and television people, magicians, preachers, and any number of other observers . . . including me. It was almost invariably concluded by the witnesses that the vexations could not have been the result of trickery by the nineteen-year-old Cuban shipping clerk around whom the phenomena centered. As bottles and boxes fell from shelves or moved themselves from hither to yon, even the prominent parapsychologists who studied the events closely in person were convinced that fraud could not be the explanation. Dr. J. Gaither Pratt of the University of Virginia and W. G. Roll, project director of the Psychical Research Foundation of Durham, North Carolina, have stated publicly that "There was no evidence indicating trickery."

In his presentation as chairman of a symposium entitled "The Miami Poltergeist" at the annual convention of the Parapsychological Association in New York City in September 1967, Roll said, "Several objects that we arranged crashed to the floor . . . while the shipping clerk and others were under observation. Apparently, the incidents were due to an unconscious form of psychokinesis or PK, the 'mind over matter' effect."

There is another explanation not publicly accepted in scientific circles but very strongly urged by those with spiritistic inclinations. This is the ghost, or spirit, theory. It is presumed by these adherents that an invisible spirit of some deceased person is present and eager to make his presence known, or to cause mischief or havoc, depending upon his personality and character status. In order to perform either playful pranks or acts of violence, this entity uses the psychokinetic force that comes from the body of an individual who is emotionally upset at the time. It is, of course, rare that the special combination of a person who is exuding PK force and a spirit entity capable of using it happen to get together. But when they do, all hell breaks loose!

The best evidence for this theory is that some kind of consciousness almost invariably seems to be behind poltergeist phenomena. There were many occasions at Tropication Arts when a beer mug or an ashtray shattered across the room from where everyone present was standing. If we rushed to the site of that disaster, the next disturbance was in another area of the room at the opposite pole from where we were. The operation would continue in this manner, as if a mind behind the occurrences was consciously playing jolly jokes on us. On occasion, if we would ask our invisible opponent to break something specific, it would do just what we requested. At other times when someone was there whom we particularly wanted to impress, absolutely nothing would move under its own power all the time he was in the warehouse. If a camera was trained on a possible locale of action, the activity would occur across the room. Yet cameras have followed Julio, as I reported in the Preface to this book, and bottles or dishes have flown somewhere far out of their range.

To imply that Julio's unconscious mind was actually *planning* such activities would indicate that he was suspected of having a split personality, but I saw no evidence of this. There were incidents, as time went on and the youth became more and more aware that he was the focal point of the happenings, when he learned consciously to will something to happen—and sometimes it would! Yet at first, when the poltergeist had just arrived, Julio was as frightened as anyone else when things crashed. Once, the moment after a large cardboard carton spilled itself off the top shelf of a tier, throwing its contents—plastic combs—all over the floor, I laid my hand over Julio's heart. It was beating frantically! His brow was covered with sweat and his face was pale. He gave every indication of such fear that only his manliness kept him from breaking out in tears as little Iris, the stockroom girl, so often did when the violence occurred. Everyone there was alarmed at first because this nameless force was persecuting them and they did not know when it might become dangerous to them personally. It never did. Julio reacted, however, with the same apprehension shown by everyone else.

On another occasion when a shot glass fell on the cement floor just behind him, Julio leaped into the air and dropped the broom and dustpan he was carrying. Once again I put my hand on his heart and its tremendous pounding indicated to me that he could not have consciously instigated the occurrence that had so startled him.

Whether or not at a later date Julio occasionally caused things to happen by concentrating on them, it certainly must have been an unconscious process most of the time. The power of the human mind is such a little-known force that we cannot say why or how this sort of thing is possible. We only know from close observation that it does occur, and that something we term "supernormal" results. When I say supernormal I am not intimating that the occurrences are beyond natural laws, but only beyond the natural laws that we as yet comprehend. Today, of course, we do not claim that we know all the laws that govern our universe. Few persons are that naïve.

Whatever this "something" is that causes a poltergeist, in attaching itself to Julio Vasquez it has played havoc with his life. He has become afraid of it and of what it occasionally causes him to do. Yet he is also reluctant to have an exorcism or any of the countless other things suggested as possible aids to rid him of it. After all, who knows any more about what it really is than he does?

Up until very recently I know he was enjoying it, after he once got over his fear. Certainly he delighted in the small amount of fame it brought him. Yet no personal publicity could make up for the terrible things that have happened to this young man.

I have watched over him as closely as possible—and that has not been at all easy—from the time the unusual manifestations first began while he was at Tropication Arts. I have observed how living with the peculiar and unusual handicap of a built-in poltergeist has affected the youth's life. It has been a fascinating story, to say the least, but seldom a happy one for him.

The history of his experiences since Tropication Arts begins before that episode ended, during the last few days Julio was employed there. When I arrived at the warehouse on Wednesday morning, February 1, police cars were outside the front door.

"Oh-oh, has the poltergeist caused some new trouble?" I wondered hopefully with exuberant apprehension and a cheerful ringing of alarm bells in my mind. That poltergeist was the most interesting thing I had ever observed, and my feelings were "the more the merrier" as far as it was concerned. It was soon revealed, however, that this was a geist in a different guise. Someone had robbed the place during the night.

When the stockroom boys, Julio and Orlando, had locked up the evening before, they had found that, in some unknown (?) way, the burglar alarm had been torn out by the roots; and so it had not been set. In the middle of the night the police discerned as they drove up the alley back of 54th Street that the warehouse door had been broken open. When Al Laubheim, the manager, arrived in answer to their call, they discovered inside little piles of burned newspaper here and there on the floor throughout the building. (This has never been explained except as something with possible voodoo or evil-spell implications.) Besides these piles of charred paper, it was found that an old portable typewriter, Al's movie camera, a few of the more expensive items of costume jewelry, and some petty cash had been stolen.

The fact that a key had been used to open a cabinet where the typewriter and cash were kept, and that the key had been returned to its hiding place, indicated that it was definitely an inside job. Neighbors told the police that they had seen at the alley door a small blue car, similar to the one that was parked near there every day; and two young men had been observed coming out of the warehouse carrying a box. The automobile was obviously Julio's Vauxhall, which he parked in back when he was at work. Police went to his home and found the car radiator warm at three o'clock in the morning; but nobody answered the door of the house Julio shared with a friend, although the police thought they saw someone peering out from behind the curtains.

The next morning Julio was at work as usual. He denied having anything to do with breaking and entering the warehouse, but he was definitely listless and ill-at-ease all day. The poltergeist continued performing, although it did nothing spectacular. The following morning Julio did not come to work and there was nothing at all zinging around the warehouse. A detective did arrive, however, because Al had called the police department and complained that they were not doing anything to retrieve his possessions. The policemen who had investigated the poltergeist, and there had been many of them around from time to time, had all been intelligent and polite. But now we were to be treated to a new brand of service.

I had never had any personal experience before with a detective; but I had seen the allegedly typical flatfoot in movies and television shows. I had also read about such persons, but I had never believed they were real. They are real. It was a detective just as flat-footed and lame-brained as any ever depicted in any two-bit thriller who barged into Tropication Arts a few minutes after twelve o'clock on Thursday, and the first thing he did was to complain because nobody was there except Glen Lewis, Al's partner, and me. The fact that it was noontime escaped him completely. After he had raged about it for a while, I mentioned casually that people around there usually went to lunch that time of day. This was *no* excuse! One got the feeling that when that great police sergeant dropped in unexpectedly, no matter what time of day, he expected all the important people to be there, lined up at the door to greet him, preferably saluting. And he seemed to think that "this did *not* include some dumb broad who claimed to be a psychical researcher, whatever the hell that was, and wanted to tell him that poltergeists, whatever *they* are, for Chri'sakes, could cause a boy to act mixed-up and do peculiar things. This was surely a ghost-happy, spook-dizzy dame who should be led away quietly."

If Julio had robbed the warehouse, it was obvious to me that he was confused or he would not have left so many clues pointing directly to him. I wanted the disgruntled cop to understand from the outset that the boy he would have to deal with was no habitual criminal. When anyone has had dishes and boxes chasing him around for three weeks, he can hardly help being in a somewhat disturbed state; but this does not make him a crook.

None of us could ever get this through to the thick-skulled gendarme, however. "I'm not here to learn about ghosts," he said with scorn. "I don't believe in ghosts. If you do, that's your business, not mine. I'm here to see about a robbery." He later told Al, "Those things you describe can't happen. I have more brains than to believe such stuff."

This sergeant took Julio with him when the boy arrived at work in the afternoon, and according to what we were later told, he browbeat him for hours. I do not hold with thievery, but then again, neither do I condone a detective's verbally torturing an emotional nineteen-year-old with the false suggestion that his mother had been left in Cuba deliberately because she was an unworthy person. Julio cried when he and I were together on Friday, as he told me things the detective had implied about his mother. The man admitted this later, so I am not depending entirely upon Julio's statement for it.

It was Friday morning that I learned the worst. When I turned on my bedside radio upon awakening, I heard that the big warehouse mystery had been solved. The spook at Tropication Arts, it was said, was none other than a young stockroom employee who confessed to doing it all with a network of threads. I rushed for the newspapers and my worst fears were realized. We would never be able to get a factual version of the situation to the public now, because "the police had unmasked the phantom of the stockroom." The mysterious poltergeist who had "baffled detectives and spookhunters" had confessed to a simple trick. "Slender threads placed at strategic places toppled boxes and glasses from the shelves." Also, "at times, the items were stacked at angles so that vibrations from jets passing overhead could set them flying."

Can you imagine those sturdy shelves in that solidly constructed warehouse sending something flying because of a vibrating overhead jet? Those shelves had been shaken with all the strength at the command of strong policemen before an object that we had deliberately placed on the edge of a shelf as a test would fall from it. Also, our close and constant supervision and investigation would have revealed a single thread on a shelf, let alone a network of them. But no one would believe us now. The newspaper was happy to state that the teenager had said it was easy to fool magicians, police, scientists, *et al.* He didn't even "have to be in the immediate vicinity when the 'poltergeist' sent things flying." With his network of threads, he could be out of sight, he had told the sergeant, who had blithely revealed his successful sleuthing to the world. It is always pleasing for police and newspapers and, for that matter, all those who think that any seemingly supernatural stories are balderdash to be able to write finis to a confusing case; and if "experts" can be stumped at the same time, that is genuinely happiness-making for them.

It is not odd that the detective had been so unenlightened as to accept that version. He had not even been willing to walk through the stockroom to observe the site of activity. That the Miami *Herald* had been taken in is what was unbelievable, for several of its reporters and cameramen were there when activity occurred, and they had expressed themselves as befuddled. Certainly there was a question in their minds as to whether or not the easy solution was the correct one. Yet to this day the *Herald* has refused to allow anyone to give Miamians the truth through their columns.

I immediately telephoned W. G. Roll at the Psychical Research Foundation in Durham. He had been trying for some time to get Julio to go to Dr. Jack Kapchan, a psychologist on the staff of the University of Miami. Dr. Kapchan, who had studied at Duke Medical School and had spent some time in the Parapsychology Laboratory, had been invited to Tropication Arts during the height of the activity and had seen phenomena he felt to be interesting and challenging. Roll told me that now that Julio was in trouble with the police it was more important than ever that I get him to the psychiatrist, and that I must not let him out of my sight until he went there. I made an appointment with Jack Kapchan for five o'clock that evening, and when I met Julio at the warehouse he promised to accompany me.

Before I had arrived that morning, I learned, Al Laubheim had made an appointment with the Miami *Herald* for Julio because the boy wanted to attest publicly that he had not caused the poltergeist activity—at least not consciously. I could not let him get away from me for fear he might not return to keep his date with the doctor, so I accompanied Julio to the *Herald* office. He was interviewed by a charming young woman, who was not charming at all in the story she wrote because she checked it with the detective before it was published. He told her that Julio had taken a lie-detector test and had admitted being the ghost and also pulling the robbery. The boy also at the same time "admitted" that he was undergoing psychiatric treatment at Jackson Memorial Hospital. This was as big a whopper as that business about the network of threads and the low-flying jets. Don't they say that a person who is so mixed-up he believes what he is saying can fool a polygraph? If, indeed, there ever was a polygraph.

Al Laubheim says that Julio and the police sergeant were in his office together the morning after the article appeared. The boy stood up to his accuser and told him right to his face that he was lying. Julio insisted he had not confessed to causing the poltergeist activity consciously and that it was an out-and-out fabrication.

"The shamus did not deny it," Al says. "He just got red in the face."

Well, whatever the truth of the matter was, it was the detective's account of it that the newspaper accepted. His conclusion, the article stated, was that the boy was "sick."

After his interview with Julio that evening, Dr. Jack Kapchan told me something quite different. He said: "I do not think that he is a severely emotionally disturbed boy. A great deal of his confusion seems to be the result of the strange occurrences around him, and the way he has been treated recently, rather than any long-standing chronic disorder."

Dr. Kaplan concluded that he thought the boy instinctively wanted to get caught, that he had a subconscious longing for discipline and perhaps was trying without realizing it to do something to get himself into trouble.

A few days after he saw Dr. Kapchan, Julio let me put him on a plane for Durham. He had lost his job by then, and the charges against him were dropped. Julio was so wishy-washy about going to North Carolina that it had been difficult to know what he planned to do. He would tell me definitely that he would go, but after talking to his Cuban friends at night, he would return in the morning convinced that it would be unwise. And I think he was particularly averse to leaving his girl, Maria, even though he knew that the Psychical Research Foundation planned to pay all his expenses and reimburse him for his time. It was not until I walked him out to the plane that I was sure

Julio was really on his way. He remained in Durham several weeks, and I have previously reported most of the findings and events of his stay. I will quote Bill Roll here in a brief recapitulation of the results.

Roll said that in an attempt to discover psychological or physiological factors that might be related to such unusually strong psychokinetic (PK) powers as were exhibited in the poltergeist activities in Miami, many tests were given Julio. No abnormal physical conditions were found and his EEG (brain wave) patterns were normal. However, the psychological tests revealed repressed feelings of hostility toward parental figures. It appears he regards employers as such figures and that the poltergeist disturbances are an *unconscious* means to express the hostility which could find no other outlet.

"In the course of the investigations in Durham," Roll stated, "studies were also carried out at the Foundation for Research in the Nature of Man, which is headed by Dr. J. B. Rhine. The young man was tested on several PK machines, including a mechanical dice release, on which he produced statistically significant results." This means that his conscious desire that the dice fall a certain way resulted in success more times than chance expectancy. Roll concluded, "Evidently, he could, to some extent, bring his PK powers under conscious control."

The transparent, plastic, rotating container with two dice, called the PK machine, broke down and the bottom lid came off while Julio was being tested. Julio had not had any possible opportunity to interfere normally with it; yet it seems just as certain that mentally he had something to do with its breakdown. The incident probably set the parapsychologists energetically trying to figure out the odds on its chance occurrence.

In addition, while Julio was in this room being tested he became irritable. He obviously felt tired and put upon, and had begun to think they were overdoing his mental exertion. At that moment a vase fell off a table outside in the hall and broke. Need I note that there was no one else in the building at the time except Julio and the researchers in the room with him? No wires, no threads, no nothing!

When the Cuban boy returned from Durham he applied for work at a national chain shoestore on North Miami Avenue. Mr. John Powers is the manager of this store, whose New York directors prefer that it remain nameless in the records. Powers' wife, Kay, is in the store with him much of the time. Julio started to work on April 20, 1967, and left April 27. He returned to pick up his last check on May 5. In Mr. and Mrs. Powers' report it is revealed once again that it was a matter of surprise to the manager of the store when things began to happen that could not be explained. Naturally everyone at first attempted to find normal answers. Then trickery was suspected. After a few days it occurred to the Powerses that the kind of funny business going on there was similar to what they had read about in the papers a few months before. They asked Julio if he was the same boy and he admitted he was, but he assured them he was not deliberately causing anything to break in their store. They finally became convinced that he was right, for they had several opportunities to realize that the youth was not near the scene of activity.

John Powers told me: "The first thing that happened in the store that was strange was while I was talking to my wife on the telephone. We have a fire extinguisher that weighs about fifteen pounds hanging on a hook on the wall. You would have to lift it in order to take it off the hook, but it fell to the floor. I do not know if Julio was near it or not. He had not been working there long, and my first impression was that the new man was probably fooling with it and didn't want to tell me."

The shoestore is about thirty feet wide. The front section is sixty feet deep, then there is a small partitioned-off area used as an office, and the room back of that is thirty feet deep. There is shelving across the middle of the back room and along all the walls. There is an upstairs storeroom, but nothing ever happened there that was unusual. On a table in the back room are a num-

ber of whiskey shot glasses that are used to hold dye when shoes
are tinted for a customer. One day one of these jiggers broke. It
was found on the floor halfway across the room from where it
normally was kept. There were shoe shelves in between that
went from the floor almost to the ceiling, so, Mr. Powers says, the
glass could not have flown or been thrown over it. Nobody was
in the back room at the time the glass fell. There is a back door,
but it is always locked and barred.

After that shot glasses kept popping all over the place. The
floor is asphalt tile and sometimes a glass would fall and not
break, but usually they were completely shattered. Those readers who are familiar with my earlier account will recall that jiggers were also a particular favorite of the geist at Tropication
Arts. By the time seven or eight of them had broken, Powers
says, he and the others would look at each other and say, "There
goes another one!" On several occasions they observed that
Julio was between one or another of them and the back room at
the time the glass crashed.

I said to Mr. Powers, "Let us explore the trickery idea for a
moment. Could Julio have picked up a couple of these and
stuck them in his pocket and then walked to the space in front
of you and pitched one so that it could have fallen as it did?"

Powers answered, "Perhaps this could have occurred in some
instances. But I don't believe it could in all of them."

"Was there ever any one moment when you actually either
were with Julio or saw him at the time that anything happened?"

"Oh, yes. I remember one time in particular that I was talking
to Phil, the manager of a store down the block, and telling him
about this funny business. It was Friday evening about seven
or eight o'clock and we were standing in my store, maybe fifteen
feet from the back room. Julio was vacuuming the floor within
five feet of the door, which was in front of me. I was *between*
him and a shot glass when it crashed. Julio was at least forty feet
away from it when it happened. Phil didn't stay around too long
after that."

When John Powers decided he might have a poltergeist on his premises he assured Julio it would not cost him his job, but he wanted the truth. He said he thought it was a trick and he was determined to find out how the boy did it. Julio, with the assurance newly acquired in Durham, replied, "No, it happens when I get very upset and excited." After that everything went smoothly for a day or two, except in the little partitioned-off area between the front and back rooms. There a cigar box in which money wrappers are kept had three or four perplexing peregrinations. "It had a very strong tendency to leave the shelf on which it stayed and sail across the room," Powers said. "Then bottles of shoe polish began to fly. This is the thing that really kind of shook me with the question of how it could possibly happen, because all of my shoe polish with the exception of what is on the selling floor is kept in the upstairs storage room; but they were breaking down on the first floor where they shouldn't have been at all."

"Was Julio there?" I asked.

"Not in the back when most of the shoe polish soloed. Once Julio and Bill Duhart, the boy who helps out part time, were running shoes—putting them in their proper spots on the wall in back. They were working in the same section not more than about a foot apart from each other. A bottle of shoe polish fell from a shelf where it was not supposed to have been and shattered on the floor. I went back to see what went this time, and I said, 'Let it alone and finish the shoes and we'll clean it up later.' So the boys continued running shoes. Then, according to Duhart and Julio, with no help from anybody a box of shoes from the wall they were running fell into the shoe polish. Duhart says he did not see Julio pitch it out there and he thinks he would have observed it if he had. It fell behind them and to the right a little bit."

"Do you think Julio might have brought the bottles of polish down from upstairs and then thrown them about?"

"Well, he had plenty of chance to do that—if that was his bag.

But frankly, I don't think so. I don't believe everything I see or hear, either. I thought he was a phony when he first came to work there. So did my wife, and I think she still leans to that idea."

Mrs. Powers said, "Well, I can't help but wonder if he might not have had some kind of string that dissolved or something like that." But then she began to recall the day Duhart brought in the bag of lunch. That was something she was sure Julio could have had no part in. It was Saturday noon and Bill and the Powerses were going to remain in the store to eat. Julio was to go out for lunch. So Bill went out early and returned with a paper bag containing a sandwich and three soft drinks, for himself and Mr. and Mrs. Powers. He laid the bag on the table in the area behind the partition and returned to the shop where the employers and Julio were all waiting on customers.

"Then," Kay Powers said, "we heard an explosion. We ran back and discovered that a bottle of cola was out of the bag and shattered on the floor. We left it there and went back to our customers. In a few minutes there was another popping sound and I went back and another bottle was out of the bag and rolling on the floor, but it had not broken. I put it back in the sack and returned to the salesroom. This same thing happened twice again. Julio was up front all the time and had not touched the bag or the bottles. I picked up the bottle each time and put it back into the bag, but it fell again. We were very busy and Julio was definitely in the front of the store. He had no chance to be back there behind the partition alone."

In the back room there is a metal ashtray that weighs about five pounds, stands about two feet high, and its base, which sits flat on the floor, is about five inches wide. You can knock it over very easily if you touch it, however. Mr. Powers does not recall clearly, but he has a vague recollection that the ashtray went over once when no one was near it. When Julio told me about the shoestore escapade, however, he seemed more impressed by this big metal ashtray's movement than about anything else that had happened.

"The reason I fired Julio," said John Powers, "was because he upset two of my patrons. Two sisters who are regular customers and friends of ours came in." Julio spoke Spanish with them while he waited on them, but all of a sudden they arose, extremely upset. They stormed up to the manager, crying, "That boy, he's a devil! He's no good!"

Powers tried to pacify them and make some sense of their complaints. He finally gathered that Julio had apparently become bored because they were trying on too many shoes. He did what most shoe salesmen might like to do if they had fewer inhibitions. He put a curse on her. Mr. Powers said, "One word led to another and he finally told her, 'You either take this pair of shoes or your blood is going to flow on the floor,' or words to that effect. That's what disturbed her so. I apologized to her and told Julio to walk away, leave them alone, and say nothing." Julio went, but they were not through complaining about him. "Why, I almost slapped his face," one girl cried.

As they stormed out, one of them brushed a sale rack and knocked down a shoe. She stooped over, picked it up, and started to return it to its place, when the whole shelf fell down.

"How big a shelf is it?" I asked Mr. Powers.

"It's a metal shelf about six feet long mounted on a frame. There are three brackets," said Powers. "I put it up whenever we have a sale." He resumed his story, "I put it back up, she went to touch it again, and it fell down again! It fell three times inside of three minutes!"

"How many times had it ever fallen before?" I asked.

"Occasionally. It isn't so solid that it never falls, but it does it rarely. Whether or not it was coincidence in this particular case —when it fell three times in a row—it didn't look like it. When she left I told Julio to get his coat and that was it. The other stuff didn't make me fire him, but that curse did. And then . . ." Mr.

Powers was excited himself as he told me all this, ". . . and then, when he returned to pick up his check the next week, as soon as he walked through the door that shelf fell off the wall!"

Mrs. Powers had remained remarkably cool all through her husband's dissertation about poltergeists on his property. But now she added her own particular pet story. To her, for some reason, perhaps because it was so personal an experience, this was more interesting than anything else that had happened. She said, "Julio came in one day with his eye swollen almost shut. I asked, 'Julio, what's wrong with you?' His eye was almost closing and all red. He said, 'I have a terrible cold.' Then he asked me, 'How do you feel?' I said, 'I feel wonderful.' He looked me right in the eye. The following morning I had a head cold and my eye was almost closed—just as his had been. That is the only thing that ever really bothered me about Julio, believe it or not." I believed. I can also understand that if he had decided he had these powers to inflict curses and illnesses on people, it could make a youth begin to think he was something extra special. Perhaps Julio was riding for a fall.

My young charge called me just after he left the shoestore to tell me about some of his experiences there, and I attempted to get a report from Mr. Powers at that time. For fear that publicity might result in unwanted and damaging crowds to his store, he refused to talk to me then, although I assured them I had no intention of informing the papers. A year later he and his wife were very pleasant when I contacted them. They invited me to their home and gladly told me their story, still simply fascinated about the whole adventure that had befallen them. It was the same kind of enchantment that had Al Laubheim and all the rest of us enthralled at Tropication Arts. It is an excitement that gives one a conversation piece for a lifetime—as you argue with friends and acquaintances about whether or not you were mesmerized, mass-hypnotized, or merely stupid to have allowed a prankster to convince you he was actually causing objects to fly with nothing else but the force of his mind! As all of us who have participated in poltergeist phenomena agree, it is truly like living in fantasyland. Imagine being the boy who has it with him all the time!

Julio reported to me just after he had left a job at the Kress Store on Flagler, the main street in downtown Miami. He admitted that funny things had gone on there, too. I immediately went to interview Barney Garner, the manager of the Kress stockroom. He told me calmly and statistically that Julio came to work for him on June 19, 1967, and left of his own accord on July 7. He had been there for five days before anything unusual occurred.

"After that did you notice anything strange?" I asked him.

"Objects started flying," he replied, still composed, almost as if he had taken it all as a matter of course. When he and his helpers were searching madly for the cause of the activity, however, it had not been quite so serene around there. Bottles of a certain insecticide had started exploding, although the store had carried that brand for years with no previous unseemly conduct on its part.

Garner showed me around the warehouse where all the supplies for the Kress store are kept. The building extends an entire block from front to back. The stockrooms, on the third and fourth floors, are the same size as the store below. They consist of hundreds of tall rows or tiers of shelves, called departments, all painted a dark mahogany and carefully labeled and indexed. The well-organized shelves are known as "bins." I must say the order and dignity of this warehouse was a revelation to me. To see behind the scenes sometimes helps one to understand how a large business manages to keep itself functioning smoothly.

Mr. Garner showed me where the insecticides were kept, and just where the bottles had crash-landed. We measured the distance carefully and it was sixteen feet away, going around the ends of the departments. It would have been impossible for anything to go through the tiers of shelves, which are all enclosed. And they extend from floor to ceiling.

"Where were you when the bottles exploded?" I asked Garner. "And where was Julio?"

"I was about twenty-five feet away, and he was about the same distance away, within my line of vision. He was nowhere near the insecticides."

"At that time you naturally did not connect him with the incident, did you?"

"No. I didn't know who he was or what was going on here. That first afternoon two bottles of insecticides crashed and the following morning another crashed. I looked at the bins and departments carefully, but there was nothing that could have propelled them. We gave everything a thorough going over immediately after each explosion occurred. We did not suspect anyone of having done it, but we made every effort to find out what could have caused it to happen. If there had been any strings or threads or anything else there we would have seen them. And Julio was not close enough to have removed anything incriminating before we got there. That is certain."

"Was Julio nervous or distraught about anything at the time?" I asked.

"He seemed a little upset. I don't think he really liked this kind of work."

Barney Garner did not associate the capricious insecticides with the new stockclerk at that time, nor did he think of it as a possible poltergeist put-on. It was not until the next week that things really began to cut loose at the Kress warehouse. In the toilet goods department, about fifty feet away from the area where the insecticides are kept, two pint-size bottles of hand lotion removed themselves and went their separate ways in another aisle two departments across the room. When the manager heard this smashup and investigated, he began to suspect some individual of pranking, and he immediately checked who was present among his employees and in what positions they were to be found. He discovered them all to be standing alert with heads tilted listening to the sound of glass breaking, wondering what was going on . . . all but Julio. Julio was not even there. He was down on the main selling floor at the time.

Later, after the Cuban boy returned to the scene, four jars of Vaseline did an invisible take-off and fell in the aisle. Then some bottles of brown shoe polish achieved a distance of forty feet away from their department, and around a corner! Standing at the end of the aisle from which the shoe polish had been invisibly projected were four or five people—depending on whose testimony we take. This slight discrepancy of one porter is the only divergence I noted in the three statements I received of the events in this store. Garner recalled that Thelma Butterfoss, Julio, and a porter were standing with him. Miss Butterfoss mentioned the same names, but she thought two porters were there—Donald and Corey. Julio agreed with her. All testimonies assure us that Julio was standing right beside the rest of the people when the commotion occurred.

Thelma Butterfoss has worked at that Kress store for almost twenty years. Never in all that time did anything aviate of its own accord until Julio Vasquez went to work there. About the big shoe polish episode—Thelma herself knows that no one could have thrown the bottles, pushed them, pulled them, or in any other way mechanically caused the happening, because everyone in the entire room was standing right beside her at the end of the aisle. When the group heard the shattering glass, they all rushed toward it together and found freshly spilled shoe polish running all over the place, Thelma said.

On the fourth floor where a lot of china is stored, at least four cups were broken. Mr. Garner does not think anyone was up there at the time it occurred. As he recalled it—I was unable to interview the young woman involved—one of the girls was coming up in the elevator and heard the loud crunch as the cups hit the floor. She investigated and found the pile of shards, smashed into the same type of small fragments everything seemed to achieve at the Kress store when the poltergeist hit. Julio was working in the hardware area on the floor below when the cups caromed about.

That was the day the new stockboy quit. Julio seemed to realize that he was getting restless and that it would not be wise for him to remain around there. It is odd that not one employer ever threatened to fire Julio when he became aware that the boy was the cause of the phenomena. I think personally that they were too intrigued with the mystery of what was going on and the challenge to learn how it operated. Perhaps each of us involved thought at one time or another that we would be able to explode the myth and reveal the great secret. As each in turn began to understand that this was not possible because we were obviously dealing with some inexplicable force, we then wanted it to linger so that we could observe as many manifestations as possible. I am positive everyone felt as I did about it. Al Laubheim, Barney Garner, and John Powers all confessed to me that they did. We wished to see more and more of the curiosities, hoping with each new episode that we might somehow get the clue that would lead us to a rational solution.

Since Julio quit working at the Kress store he has had a number of jobs. Poltergeist activity has been sporadic because he has learned to stop working before conditions begin to upset him. This has kept him financially insecure, but emotionally out of trouble.

In early June 1968, Julio married Maria Santos, the sweet young girl who had stood by him so faithfully through all his vicissitudes. Later in the summer Maria told me that shortly after they were married she and Julio had a little spat. He was carrying a tray in his hands and laid it on the counter in the kitchen. Then he went into the living room and threw himself down on the bed. His new wife stepped into the kitchen a few moments later and a shot glass on the tray exploded in front of her. Fortunately it did not hurt her, but it gave her a healthy respect for her husband's poltergeist.

When I talked to them before Christmas I learned that Julio was blissfully anticipating becoming a father. He was sure psychically that it would be a boy—but this time he was wrong. On February 22, 1969, Irma Leonor was born; and Julio found out that a daughter was just as exhilarating as a son could have been. He and Maria were the happiest they had ever been in their lives.

On the night of March 3, 1969, less than two weeks after his daughter's birth, Julio was working at the Star Service Station in the heart of the largest Negro housing area in Miami. At about 8:30 two young thugs with gun in hand arrived to stage a hold-up. As Julio saw them coming he sensed trouble for himself very strongly—but he was still not able to keep the poltergeist from taking him over. There is no other way to explain it—Julio is too intelligent to have acted as he did if his normal consciousness had been functioning. It is similar in a way to the crazy robbery at Tropication Arts that left so many clues pointing to Julio. He must get confused and the entity that is "bugging" him takes control. I do not know how else to attempt to explain what happens.

When the robbers demanded cash of him, the Cuban youth replied, "If you want the money come and get it." The sixteen-year-old boy with the gun fired at Julio's head and missed. Instead of sensibly using this reprieve to dash to safety, Julio attempted to take the gun away from the robber. A second shot hit him in the shoulder, and a third shot almost killed him. It went into his intestines, shattering his aorta and the main descending artery. He almost bled to death before the excellent surgeons at Jackson Memorial Hospital were able to save his life; but still he was given last rites by a priest. I talked to his doctor, who told me that an artificial artery segment has been used, but that he would be a very sick boy for a long time. He never will be able to do lifting and heavy work again.

Perhaps by giving him this last and most terrible of all evidence of its power over him, the poltergeist has done him a back-handed favor. At least now Julio is terribly afraid of it and willing to try in every way possible to rid himself of it.

Julio and Maria and the baby are now subsisting on Workman's Compensation of $45 per week, and he has petitioned the board for an increase. The sixteen-year-old boy who shot him was found guilty and his sentence is pending because of his youth. The Psychical Research Foundation is still as interested in Julio as ever. In the spring of 1968 they had made arrangements for a grant which would have paid for his expenses and tuition if he would attend the Durham Technical Institute; but he refused to go to Durham. It would be of great interest for parapsychology if a young man with Julio's psychokinetic abilities could be there under observation, yet his reluctance to be a guinea pig is understandable.

The most encouraging news for Julio right now is that I was lucky enough to learn that Richard J. (Jerry) Banks, District Supervisor of the Vocational Rehabilitation Service, is not intimidated by psychical phenomena. I talked to him about Julio and his problems, and he was very interested in trying to help him. He will try to find a way to train Julio for some useful work that he will be physically capable of doing and also help him to locate a good job.

We can only hope that this time the story of Miami's Pertinacious Poltergeist can be marked finis and will not have to be continued in another book.

CHAPTER VIII

A House
of Tragedy

QUITE OFTEN a certain home may have a history of sudden death or tragic accidents involving the people who live in it or their families. When there are reports of haunting phenomena therein as well, who gets the blame for the disasters? Yes, the ghost is considered to be the culprit every time. Yet it is questionable whether a quiet, pipe-smoking spook who seldom makes his presence known can be the cause of all the violence connected with San Antonio's Brooks House. Since he apparently has been lurking there peacefully for years, perhaps it is some ghostly newcomer who causes the havoc, if, indeed, any entity is to blame.

Located in the oldest residential section of town on a lot that backs up to the charming San Antonio River, this late-Victorian-style house bears a newly acquired Official Historical Medallion reading: TEXAS HISTORIC LANDMARK. This is because it was the home of Cadet Sidney J. Brooks, Jr., for whom Brooks Air Force Base was named. In 1909 his father, the first judge of the 57th District Court, bought the house, which had been built about 1890 by the Hertzbergs, a well-known local family.

Twenty-two-year-old Cadet Brooks met his death in an airplane crash on Tuesday, November 13, 1917. It was his final flight to win his commission as a first lieutenant in America's newly formed Flying Corps. Preparatory to going overseas, the young cadet had been inoculated with anti-typhus serum on Monday, and when he left for his last test flight the next day he complained of feeling ill. Today I am sure no one would be allowed to go up when he was not well, but that early in the flight game such precautions were not taken. According to the San Antonio *Express,* Wednesday, November 14, 1917, experienced aviators who witnessed the two thousand-foot descent which ended in Brooks's crash believed that he had fainted as he started down.

In 1917 the U.S. Army had been seeking a place for an airfield where training would not be interrupted by changing climate. The area of South Texas near San Antonio offered such a setting, so a thirteen-hundred-acre site in the southeast corner of the city was chosen, and the second oldest active U.S. Air Base was born there on December 5, 1917. Sidney J. Brooks, Jr., was one of the first American cadets killed training for World War I duty, and the very first to have died at the newly formed base, so it was named for him. Brooks was posthumously awarded his lieutenancy and his pilot's wings.

Brooks Field has gone on to participate to a large degree in American military aviation history. From its first mission, the training of Army pilots, to its present role as the Free World's finest space medicine research center, Brooks has been the scene of great gains in America's conquest of the sky. If Lt. Brooks continues to exist, as certain indications in this book might presuppose him to, he cannot but be proud of the base that bears his name.

Deeds to the property on which the Brooks House is located go back as far as 1819, and it is rumored that before that time a lost Spanish mission (or early church) existed there. There is even the hint that treasure is buried on the land, either from the church's hoard or from a train robbery that occurred on the nearby railroad, or both. Why the present owners, who tend to believe these rumors, do not spend all their time outside digging has not been explained to my satisfaction.

Mr. and Mrs. Victor J. Paetznick and what is left of their family live there now, having moved into the Brooks House in 1952. Mrs. Paetznick, a pleasant, plump woman named Leta, and her daughter, Mrs. Rosamond Lane, who is forty-one and looks about twenty-five, are both strongly psychic. Even Victor has occasionally reported some mild experiences in the past. It is only since they have been here that overt manifestations have occurred in the Paetznicks' vicinity, however. And only here has catastrophe repeatedly struck the family. It began with the violent death of their oldest son, Victor Jr., on December 13, 1963.

The ghost's most prevalent indication over the years has been that odor of pipe smoke. Leta says, "I first noticed the smell of a pipe in this house when I was here alone the year we moved in. I became aware of a very strong maple-scented fragrance of tobacco when I was in the kitchen. I walked to the front of the house to see who had entered smoking a pipe, and the aroma followed me into the living room. No one had come in, so I dismissed it from my mind. By the time the rest of the family became aware of it, we had also had other ghostly manifestations. The smell of the pipe would often follow all of us through the house, quite strong at times."

Rosamond was with her mother one day when the aroma of pipe smoke went with them into the bathroom. She spoke aloud to the ghost, asserting that no gentleman should be where he was at that moment. The pipe immediately departed.

Rosamond has also smelled flowers and pine scents in the house when they would not normally have been there. Asked if she was sure it was not her imagination, she insisted it was not. She was also asked if suggestion might not play a role in something as nebulous as an odor. If someone in the house said, "I smell the pipe again," might not others have also been influenced to think they smelled it? Rosamond pointed out in rebuttal that on occasion one member of the family might declare the fragrance to be present only to have others disagree and insist it was not there at all. Also, she said, visitors have often smelled it and asked who was smoking a pipe.

Mrs. Lane's denial of the possibility of imagination playing at least a part in the haunting here does not invalidate this possibility. Nonetheless, reported events seem to be confirmed on enough occasions to make a certain amount of supernormal activity probable. From the beginning, members of the family say they checked every other known possibility to see why the aroma of pipe smoke occurred before they gave in to the idea that it might be of ghostly origin. Outlets, pipes, and vents have all been examined, in case something actually burning somewhere might be to blame.

The first time Victor Paetznick smelled the pipe smoke he went all over his home to see who or what might be causing it. He even went outside and walked all around the yard but never found any normal source for the odor. After it had occurred on a number of occasions, Victor admitted defeat and gave up. He says it is a pleasant aroma, probably from a pleasant ghost who does no harm. As far as other manifestations are concerned, Victor says, "I have never had any of the experiences with ghosts the girls have had. I did smell the pipe smoke quite a lot when we first moved in here. I've become used to it and haven't paid much attention to it lately." He has a pipe of his own but says he very seldom smokes it. Asked if he had heard footsteps in the house when no one was home but himself, Mr. Paetznick, a calm, unemotional man who works in a civil engineering capacity with the city's freeways, could not think of an occasion when he had.

Victor has realized for years that his wife was more susceptible to psychic influences that he, but he does not think she tends to overreact to her imagination. Usually when she has a premoni-

The Audubon House, Key West, Florida.

The William Lyon Mackenzie House, Toronto, Canada.

"Feeling the Vibrations!" Raji the Warlock with the piano that plays alone at night.

The home of Dr.
Kendall D. Gregory,
Gulfport, Mississippi.

Wisteria behind the
house.

Careby Hall, the home of Dr. William E. Hatcher—ghost. Fork Union, Virginia

The home of Mrs. Faye Cook,
Murray, Utah, showing the
window of the haunted attic.

Mrs. Cook greets Toni Carlin
at her front door.

Beautiful Bradmar, Denver, Colorado.

Dr. and Mrs. Robert A. Bradley before the fireplace in the drawing room.

The pregnant angels.

Service Club No. 2, U.S. Army
Medical Training Center, Fort
Sam Houston, Texas.

Sgt. Louis Milligan in the "chair
room" below the "suicide" pipes.

The Brooks House, San Antonio, Texas.

tion about something, ample evidence follows to prove that she was right.

Like the day Victor Jr., who was in the Merchant Marines, was killed. Leta had been shopping when, she told me, "All of a sudden while I was in a grocery store there was something like a heavy weight on me. I was so depressed that I felt awful and could hardly move. I asked a clerk if I might sit down, and a chair was provided for me. I must have sat there for an hour, feeling that something was terribly wrong somewhere, but not sure who it involved. I'd had similar sensations before when someone had died. Finally I decided I must make the effort to leave the store and I went to the nearby San Fernando Cathedral. I was brought up a Catholic, so now I lit a candle and sat for a long time in the church. My husband was to pick me up in town when he got off work, so I managed to get myself to our meeting place on time. It was about five-fifteen when I was telling him about how bad I felt. We later learned that it was just about this time that my son was dying on shipboard in San Francisco."

Rosamond lived in Dragerton, Utah, at the time of her brother's death. Divorced from Dr. Carel Lane, she was taking care of their four sons, Carel Jr., Richard, Dennis, and Jimmie. The boys had come home for lunch and gone back to school and she was doing the dishes when all of a sudden, she says, "I felt as if I were having a heart attack. I lay down on the couch and after a while the pain left but I started crying. I didn't know what was the matter with me. I thought I'd flipped or something. I was so blue and upset I didn't know what to do. The feeling continued until that night, when I began to think that everybody hated me. I was even afraid someone was going to kill me. Rationally I knew it was not true and was afraid I was losing my mind. Yet still, at midnight I looked out of the house before going to bed to make sure no one was out there who might shoot me. It was the next morning that Mother called to tell me she had just received word of Victor's death."

Leta said, "We are quite sure my son was murdered. We have made a number of inquiries but have never received any satisfactory details about how he died."

Rosamond drove home from Utah for her brother's funeral and arrived early Sunday afternoon. Her uncle, Paul Paetznick, came from Bucyrus, Ohio, where he is the pastor of a Lutheran church. After members of the family visited the funeral home they sat up late and talked. About 1:30 or 2:00 A.M., when everyone had finally retired, Rosamond, sleeping in the large bedroom over the front living room, was awakened by the sound of a tremendous crash. She says, "I sat up in fright, then got out of bed but couldn't see anything that might have fallen over or in any way caused the racket." Just then she heard a dog howling—a mournful, high-pitched keening—right outside her window on the upstairs side porch of the house. She knew there was no dog there, and wondered if the wail of a banshee might sound like that.

Running out into the hall, Rosamond met her uncle, who had not heard the crash but had been awakened by the howling. In the downstairs hall they bumped into Rosamond's twenty-four-year-old brother David, charging out of the living room with a gun in his hand. He had been asleep on the couch there, had heard the loud crash and the howling dog, and was ready to take care of the situation the best way he knew how. Aroused now by all the commotion, the rest of the family arrived; but no one else admitted having heard the original disturbances.

Once after Victor Jr.'s death his mother thought she heard his footsteps coming down the stairs. Nobody else was in the house at the time and Leta was just out of the bathtub, dressing in the bedroom at the front end of the hall on the first floor. She grabbed up a robe when she heard the steps. Then, suspecting that somebody had entered the house while she was in the tub, she panicked and ran to the front door.

"Afterward, as I thought about it," she said, "I recognized the steps as my dead son's. I was embarrassed that I had acted so silly about it. If I had remained calm he might have been able to reveal himself to me in some other way, maybe even talk to me." This reaction has a certain amount of muscle in it that most people would hardly be able to manage in a similar situation. In fact, it is likely that more people might have run from the possibility of a ghostly manifestation than from an intruding stranger.

The Brooks House combines various architectural influences and styles. That stairway on which footsteps are sometimes heard is quite long and steep, for all the ceilings are unusually high, even for the period in which the building was designed.

As you walk through the front door of the house there is almost the feeling that its occupants consider it a shrine because of the many huge religious paintings around. Leta is an amateur artist who prefers copying the classics to painting from life, so one wall contains a large, brilliantly colored "Sistine Madonna," another features "The Madonna and the Child," and a third has the "Madonna of the Chair." It is frankly pretty wild to walk into this house, and yet I must say the pictures make a striking and not unpleasant appearance. Leta's genuine aptitude for using her hands is more particularly in evidence in her sculptures, which show definite talent. A few of the busts and heads she has done are quite good copies of works of art; but her original heads of Rosamond's children are real delights.

Mrs. Paetznick's other major interest is reading. Lining the walls of the downstairs hall is a large library, particularly featuring a most adequate collection of psychic and occult books. She does not go so deeply into metaphysical reading, however, since a day in 1952 not long after the family moved into the Brooks House. While sitting in her comfortable lounge chair in her favorite corner between two windows in the back living room she heard a man's voice, deep and gentle, saying, "Be careful, my dear, be careful." It was a sound external to her and completely independent of her own mind. Since she was not involved in any projects at the moment about which special care need be taken, and since nothing came up very soon about which she might have been forewarned, she has decided that the admonition must have had to do with her reading. Since then she has rather restrained herself and not delved so industriously into the deeper occult tomes.

"Once some years later," Leta said, "someone upstairs called to me—when nobody was upstairs. I was alone in the house and walking down the front hall when I heard coming through the stairwell a rather high pitched voice calling, 'Leeeeeeeeeta, Leeeeeeeeta.' Now, my name is unusual. I doubt if you have heard it many times. It isn't one you would confuse with another. Neither could I doubt the reality of that voice; it was sort of singing the name—'Leeeeeeeeeta, Leeeeeeeeta.' "

Rosamond Lane has seen a few ghosts in the house. In April 1960 she was living with her parents while pregnant with Jimmie, her youngest son. She was sleeping in the same bedroom in which the crash was to occur several years later at her brother's death. It was about 2:00 A.M. when she was awakened by someone sitting down on the side of her bed. She was startled to see beside her a little old lady with gray hair, wearing a simple black dress. Rosamond had been worried because, being RH-negative, she always had trouble delivering her babies. The spectral visitor evidently knew this, for she said, "You don't have to worry. You'll have him four months from today." The next morning Rosamond wrote that date down on her calendar, and Jimmie arrived exactly on schedule, with little trouble.

Another night about a year later something shook the foot of Rosamond's bed and woke her, she says. She could see a tall man in a dark suit silhouetted against the light that was on in the hall outside her door. Being more than half asleep, she reacted to this rather peculiarly. She was not frightened, but neither was she able to observe the proper amenities in such a situation. "Oh, I can't talk now," she said to him. "I'm too tired." So he went away.

On July 9, 1967, when Jimmie was seven years old, Rosamond

and he were motoring to her parents' home for dinner when a drunken driver doing seventy miles an hour in a thirty-mile zone crashed into their car. Rosamond sustained a broken ankle and shattered heel that still cause her to limp. Jimmie had a skull fracture and numerous large lacerations all over his face and head. Fortunately, due to diligent massage with castor oil by his mother and grandmother, the scars on this alert blonde youngster's face are almost invisible today.

On Halloween of that year a few odd manifestations were observed, according to the Paetznicks. There was a heavy metal floor lamp sitting next to the front door waiting to be taken out for repair. During the afternoon, in front of Leta, Rosamond, and her oldest son, Carel, the lamp glided across the room by itself. There was no rug on the floor at the time, and if anyone had been pulling the lamp with a rope or wire it could plainly have been seen. Less visible string or thread could not have moved such a heavy object. The lamp's own cord was wrapped firmly around its base in preparation for traveling to the electrician. Later that evening when some of the neighborhood children came in for Trick or Treat, their bags of candies also slid across the floor by themselves, I was told.

These just show the sort of things a haunted house can produce on Halloween if it has a mind to. But can it really cause tragedy to the people who live there? Something in the house, at least, knew about Rosamond's most crushing blow shortly before it occurred. She and a friend, Lucille Pressett, who was visiting her from Utah, were playing with a Ouija board in June 1968. They were just fooling around, asking silly questions like "Am I going to get married again?" and "Is my daughter going to get married?" and such things. Then the board seemed to take off on a tack all its own and began to write frightening remarks such as: "Dennis needs you. Shoulder hurts. Plane crash. Hole in the ground. Head hurts. Dennis wants you. He will get killed."

Rosamond threw the Ouija aside and tried not to pay attention to such appalling statements. About a week later when she and her friend were again attempting to enjoy the Ouija's odd and provoking observations, the unhappy predictions involving her children recurred. They so unnerved Rosamond that she began to cry and her mother said, "Oh, for heaven's sake put that thing up."

It was just a few weeks later, on July 19, 1968, that Rosamond's two middle boys, Rickie and Dennis, went to visit their father in Eagle Mountain, California. He was flying them in his private plane when it crashed, killing all three of them!

After recounting the incidents that have convinced her she lives with ghosts, Leta Paetznick pulled one more plum out of her bag of remembrances. She did it reluctantly because she considered the event so unpleasant. From another point of view it is also mildly hilarious.

One night a strange man tried to get into Leta's bed. It happened in that big downstairs bedroom—she says she would not sleep there again if you paid her to. The intruder sported a little moustache and looked exactly like a descendant of an early owner of Brooks House. For this reason she suspects it was this ancestor himself. As he put his knee on the side of her bed and started to get under the covers she sat up indignantly, pointed her hand dramatically at the door, and shouted, "Out!" He left. This is what inclines one to agree with Leta that he must have been a ghost. Surely a housebreaker or an amorous living suitor would not have been deterred so easily.

CHAPTER IX

The Hut
in the Brush

TRADITIONALLY, a haunted house should be empty, lonely, a bit worn and dilapidated, and, if possible, of an unusual size and shape. If it can sit on a slight elevation, surrounded by gaunt trees—all the better. But how many of our really interesting ghostly retreats have filled this bill? Very few, in fact.

In Virginia I discovered exactly such a house, reposing in lonely isolation on a hill above Fork Union, a small town geographically almost in the exact center of the state. Careby Hall, the home of Dr. William E. Hatcher, the founder of Fork Union Military Academy, glimmers palely through the trees by day and is even more spectrally effective as it shines in the dark by reflected moonlight. When it is visited it rejects one with that hollow-eyed vacant stare that only a plethora of uncurtained windows can produce. Even its unusual lopsided construction— a round tower on the right, dormer windows and a porchless front entrance in the center, a gabled roof over square-shaped rooms on the left—gives it the austerity a proper haunted house should have. A slight list to starboard and general disrepair add to its forlorn and defenseless aspect. A house like this was made for warm hearth fires and busy, bustling inhabitants. For it to be sitting starkly alone and untended seems unfair and unkind—but certainly and very definitely ghostly.

This eleven-room structure did not always have the lean and hungry look of a place that time has forgotten. Once it was a happy, sociable home where an energetic family was raised, and the center of jolly campus parties and friendly gatherings at the feet of the eminent minister who built it in 1897 and lived in it until his death at the age of seventy-eight in 1912.

When I was driven up the hill by Capt. Kenneth Hardesty of Fork Union Military Academy to see Careby Hall it was in November and there was an early snow on the ground. The bare trees in the grove surrounding the house were shivering, and the house itself looked as if it were cringing from the unseasonal cold. We were unable to go inside, but wandered around looking at the forbidding exterior as long as the penetrating wind would allow. I knew nothing about this house except its reputation for being haunted, yet I called Ken Hardesty's attention to an upper-right-hand window in the tower. I did not think I actually *saw* anything looking out of it, but I had a very strong feeling that something was watching us from there. I was later to learn that at least six people associated with the Academy have either seen an apparition looking from this window or experienced something else of a curious nature involving it.

Capt. Robert K. Spencer later told me that this window was in what might be considered the attic, a portion of which had been made into a small reading room or study. From the windows one can see a great distance. Even now, scattered around all over the floor are fragments of old books and some business and personal letters—many of them in Dr. Hatcher's own handwriting. Capt. Spencer said, "Some of these that I have read give wonderful insight into the personality and character of Dr. Hatcher—a very considerate gentleman, a loving husband and father, a devout man of God, a tireless traveler and worker, a good organizer and businessman, and a generally wonderful humanitarian.

If I had lived at Careby Hall, I'm sure I would have found this the perfect spot, as he must have, for meditation, for study, and for preparing sermons."

The home is still owned by descendants of Dr. Hatcher, but none of them find it expedient to live there at the present time. It has remained vacant since the passing of the last of Dr. Hatcher's children, Mrs. Elizabeth Sadler. Bob Spencer stated that soon after his arrival at Fork Union he used to visit Careby Hall often, accompanied by cadets, to see "Ma" Sadler, as she was affectionately known to them. She enjoyed taking them on tours of the house and telling them about the old days there. Capt. Spencer particularly commented on Dr. Hatcher's study, which his daughter kept as if she were expecting him to come in at any moment. His desk and chair were there with folio of paper and pen and ink; several books were spread around; and his spectacles were open on the desk. Ma Sadler said the room was just as her father had left it. Perhaps in the days of television's "The Ghost and Mrs. Muir," the idea does not sound as impossible as it once did, so may I suggest that from time to time the good minister used to drop in to read a favorite book or go over his accounts? Now that this den is no longer furnished, he goes up to the tower and looks out the window.

Dr. William E. Hatcher came to the town of Fork Union for the first time in the summer of 1864. He was then the pastor of the Bainbridge Street Baptist Church of Manchester, Virginia, and had been invited to conduct a one-week revival meeting at the local Fork Baptist Church. He achieved success during that week, not only as a revivalist but as a suitor, for he met the true love of his life there. He and Miss Virginia Snead were married on December 22 of that year.

When Dr. Hatcher later became pastor of Grace Street Baptist Church in Richmond, about fifty miles away, he and his wife and children visited her relatives at Fork Union every summer. Finally, in 1896, he decided to build a country summer home at Fork Union as a place of retreat for himself and his family. He bought twenty-six acres of hilly land and built on the most symmetrical elevation. When the house was completed, he named it Careby Hall after the Hatcher ancestral home in Lincolnshire, England.

Being a great socializer, Dr. Hatcher continually invited friends to visit his new place in the country. Knowing him, they were willing to take the risk that the "hut in the brush" to which he invited them would not be quite the rural structure he depicted. Every summer the house was made lively with numerous guests from all over the South, many of them fellow Baptist ministers, who are noted for their spirited gatherings.

The Sabre, Fork Union Military Academy's newspaper, tells how the Academy came into being.

"After retiring from the ministry, Dr. Hatcher made his summer residence into a permanent, year-round home. Looking across from Careby Hall to a gently rising slope, he could see a magnificent grove of oaks and kept thinking it would be a 'splendid place for a school.'" After voicing these sentiments occasionally, Dr. Hatcher convinced himself it was worth some effort on his part to accomplish. He twisted the arms of ten of his friends to make a loan of fifty dollars each to establish a school for college preparation with a five-hundred-dollar endowment. With this money, Dr. Hatcher proposed to secure a teacher and schoolhouse in the village to use until more funds could be acquired for building construction.

On October 15, 1898, Fork Union Academy opened its doors to nineteen boys and girls from the local area. Dr. Hatcher was elected to the post that eventually became known as the President of the Board of Trustees. At the beginning of the 1902–03 session, the school became known as Fork Union Military Academy. Today it is a nonprofit institution owned by the Baptist General Association of Virginia, fully accredited as a Military Preparatory School with highest rating.

In Careby Hall members of the Academy's new Psychic Science Club are offered the unique experience of having right on their own campus a haunted house to investigate to their hearts' content. They have already had some interesting results. Two cadets presently at the academy, seventeen-year-old John M. Sioris of Silver Spring, Maryland, and sixteen-year-old Felix Rexach of San Juan, Puerto Rico, made an expedition to the house one night in March 1969. Since they could not get in, for it is kept carefully locked, they shined their flashlight all over the exterior of the house and into the windows.

If a ghost alone in such a house became aware that he was suddenly receiving unusual attention, would he not most likely endeavor to make his presence known? The ghost of Careby Hall did exactly this by whistling. The cadets definitely heard someone whistling a tune inside the house. It was unfamiliar to them and sounded, they said, "like an old tune ... something like a waltz. ..." The whistling came from the upper-right window of the front of the tower. That same one I mentioned earlier.

The year before the Psychic Science Club was formed, Cadet Karl Woelfel of Miami, Florida, went for an off-the-record visit to the house with two other football players. They discovered that there was an assailable secret window that might be pried open, and so they entered the building. This does not preclude the possibility that someone else may also have entered the same way and was secreted there. However, in such a small community and such an isolated house, it hardly seems probable that anyone would have been hiding out there on as many occasions as visitors have reported hearing noises or seeing ghostly manifestations in the house. Just before this was written Capt. Spencer reported to me that he had been inside the building on an inspection tour and there was no evidence whatever that it had been used for a hideout at any time.

Cadet Woelfel and the other two boys entered the house and were looking it over. They had gone through the six downstairs rooms and were standing in the spacious entrance hall near the beautiful solid-oak staircase looking at its intricate carvings, when all three heard a noise from upstairs. It was apparently not an easy-to-describe noise, because the cadets were completely unable to agree on exactly what it sounded like; but it was definitely not the kind that should be heard in an uninhabited house. It was real and solid and earthy. The youths hastily scrambled back through the window, having no desire to confront either man or ghost under such inauspicious circumstances. About twenty feet from the house they stopped running and stood and looked back. Then, Woelfel says, "We all noticed that the window upstairs on the right was open and a dim glow was visible there. It was distinctly a presence of some kind, but one that seemed to be made of fog or smoke."

It has been said in that community for many years, particularly among the Negroes, that the old Hatcher home was haunted. Capt. Spencer talked to an elderly man who is employed by the school at present and has been familiar with Careby Hall, the Academy, and environs for many years. His name is Wyatt "Cracker" Bryant. Bob said, "Cracker told me that one night many years ago he was attracted by a pack of small yelping dogs and puppies on one of the roads leading to the Hatcher place. He said that the dogs seemed to be jumping up at someone who was there other than he, but he could see no one. He could see only the dogs jumping up and standing on their hind legs around 'something.' "

Cracker Bryant also recalled that about twenty-five years ago one night a group of the boys were having a 'possum hunt in the woods near Careby Hall. The dogs treed a 'possum right in front of the old house and the hunters gathered around the trunk with the yelping dogs. Just then the whole group saw a ghostly figure standing at the upstairs-right window intently watching what was going on. Some of the men said the figure looked like Dr. Hatcher.

The Psychic Science Club has been collecting accounts of the haunting for its records. Organized in the spring of 1968, it has proved to be one of the most popular extra-curricular activities on the campus. Capt. Hardesty and Capt. Spencer started the club because of their own personal interest in the subject and their conviction that it was shared by many of the students. Their faith in this concept was rewarded by a membership that from the beginning has filled all available meeting places to capacity. The goals of the club have been established as "The desire to promote serious discussion and study of the now well-established field of psychical research, because this area of man's increasing knowledge about himself and the hitherto unrealized and unexplored qualities of his mind is becoming a subject of interest and importance in every circle of our culture."

I was invited to Fork Union in November 1968 to address the Psychic Science Club, but interest in my subject was such that the entire student body and most of the faculty and their wives—numbering approximately eight hundred persons—turned out for the lecture. It was then that I learned that the campus not only had many enthusiastic cadets, but also a haunted house for this book.

Psychic Science Club members have been investigating Careby Hall unofficially since then in an attempt to acquire evidence for me. It is curious, however, that the only time Dr. Hatcher was actually seen and identified on the campus was not in his old home. Of course, he must have affection also for the main administration and classroom building of the Academy, for it is named Hatcher Hall, and its lobby contains a large portrait of him.

This incident occurred about eight years ago, and the cadet who reported it to Capt. Spencer revealed by his straightforward account that he was not seeking attention or notoriety, he was merely stating an unusual occurrence. This young man had pulled guard duty and had to spend the night in the guard room in Hatcher Hall. After he had checked the entire campus, he returned to Hatcher Hall and extinguished all lights in the building except the one in the guard room. Then he prepared to retire. Just then he heard what sounded like a door opening and closing on the second floor. Shining his flashlight before him, the cadet went up the stairs, opened the large door onto the main hall, and observed that the hall was totally dark. He walked a short distance back and forth, shining his torch all about. Just then the cadet felt something brush up against him, and he turned abruptly and flashed his light behind him. He was astounded when its glow revealed an elderly man with a gray beard, wearing a black overcoat and Homburg and carrying a cane or umbrella. The old gentleman did not stop to pass the time of night. He walked with a sprightly step down the hall and disappeared. And his face was a duplicate of the face in the large painting of Dr. Hatcher in the entrance hall.

The most recent report comes from two cadets, Malcolm W. Smith of Laurel, Maryland, and Alex P. Woskob of State College, Pennsylvania, who went into the house one night in April 1969. While standing near one of the nine fireplaces, both became conscious of something beside them. They did not actually see a phantom, but they felt his presence strongly; and they also heard a sound like shuffling feet on the floor near them. These two cadets left quickly.

It is to be hoped that the Psychic Science Club will continue its interest in Careby Hall, and will organize an occasional séance or development circle to meet there and attempt to learn what can be manifested by Dr. Hatcher and any of his invisible cohorts. Insistently maintained rumors, such as the one that some students have tried to open the front door only to have it pushed shut in their faces, must be tested under controlled conditions. It has already been ascertained that there are no springs on the door that would normally force it to resist being opened. Now they will have to learn if any other natural pressures can be at work, and if not they will have to institute a stakeout to observe the door under any and all possible conditions. If there is then evidence that the resistance is more than a rumor, some gains for the "cause" of psychical research will have been made.

Careby Hall thus will have a continuing role to play on the campus. It will not be considered as simply a relic of the past.

This is why plans for a restoration that are now under way, supervised by a local contractor, Alex W. Leland, were not received with any joy by Psychic Science Club members. Although they share with other cadets and faculty members at the Academy the desire to see lights shine again from the windows of Careby Hall, they are not in any hurry for this to happen. They want first to give Dr. Hatcher the opportunity to attempt to prove in any way possible to him that he does still survive and is interested in his home and his school.

So far he has not been doing too bad a job of it.

CHAPTER X

Only You May See
My Face

"I DON'T MIND getting poison-pen letters," said Tom Carlin of Salt Lake City's Radio Station KSXX, "but . . . from a *dead* man?"

Faye Cook, the woman who lives in the house where Carlin received his venomous message, is not alarmed at all about her unseen visitor.

"As long as we leave each other alone," she told me, "I'm not afraid of living in a house that has a ghost in the attic. He stays upstairs and we live in the house below. It works out very well." In fact, recently he has been of such service to her that she has almost begun to consider him affectionately. Still, he is welcome to leave any time.

It is obvious that in Mrs. Cook we have a woman who is complacent about her problem. Whether or not the ghost in her home in Murray, Utah, is a long-term asset will have to be determined by his future behavior. So far he has definitely been worth his keep. If a ghost can be domesticated, having unseen eyes and ears about the place with a certain ability to foresee the future is not to be despised.

The territory where Mrs. Cook lives is one of the most spectacularly beautiful in all of the United States. Back of Salt Lake City the Wasatch Mountains tower with immediacy. They do not slope and amble up to the city. They are right there, looming benignly like church spires. When Brigham Young first stepped through a pass in these mountains and saw the entire Salt Lake Valley spread out below him, he said, "This is the place." With a combination of prayerful faith and hard work the Mormons then turned the foothills of the mountains into a city that is clean, well managed, and beautiful. They irrigated the entire area so thoroughly that flowers bloom there more luxuriously than anywhere else except a few coastal regions of this country. Murray, a suburb just south of Salt Lake City, is where Faye Cook's funny little old house is located. She first saw the house in 1936 and knew by some kind of prescience that she would eventually live in it. It was none of her doing, however, when the move finally came about.

In 1945 Faye and her husband had been searching all over the Salt Lake Valley for a home to buy. Their to-be-haunted house had not been put up for sale until the day before its ad appeared; and when Mr. Cook saw the description of it in the Salt Lake *Tribune* he felt sure it was just what he was looking for. As soon as he finished his breakfast he drove out to see it, and in no time at all he had deposited $400 as a down payment. He returned home and told his wife about it, and a few days later they moved in.

Although she had been impressed by the flickering shadows cast by the kitchen range when she was first there and had somehow known she was to return to live there, when Mrs. Cook saw the house the second time she was appalled.

"I couldn't believe that anything could be done to make it livable," she told me. "There was teavine growing all over the yard, even through the cracks in the floors and walls. There was a hole in the front yard that you could have buried a car in, and there were wild plum bushes growing where we now have the chain-link fence."

Mr. and Mrs. Cook have worked hard to improve the property and now have a nice lawn. They also have added a small room onto the east side of the kitchen, where Faye's mother sleeps. (Neither Faye's mother nor her husband, incidentally, care a thing about pursuing ghostly topics. Both of them have had experiences in the house they cannot fathom, and they want no more. They think it is wise to leave well-enough alone. Fortunately for this narrative, Mrs. Cook and her twenty-four-year-old son Gordan are interested in trying to get to the root of the matter, and so they have encouraged the manifestations.)

With all their efforts to improve it, the house still looks small and aged. The plaster is flaking and the eaves drip with spider webs, yet there is a coziness about the place that indicates that someone who cares lives there. It is the attic of this house that is shared with the haunt.

Mrs. Cook told me that from the time they moved in, on various occasions her mother, her daughter, who is now married, and her son slept in the little attic cubbyhole. From time to time they would mention that something odd had occurred. She said, "Gordan kept telling me about strange things that happened during the night while he slept up there, but I thought it was just his imagination." Unlike some other inhabitants of ghost houses that we have visited, Mrs. Cook was not a complete skeptic when the manifestations began to bother her. Her background is Irish, Scottish, and Danish, and she has experienced psychical phenomena before, as undoubtedly had her Celtic forebears. Possibly this also accounts for the fact that she is a poet who has written as many as five hundred poems.

Her own personal contacts with the ghost developed gradually. "At first," she said, "I could hear things in the attic. Then once in a while I felt somebody or something touch me when I was all alone. It was not until May 20, 1961, that I had my first actual encounter with the ghost. I was in bed in my bedroom down-stairs, just below the attic room, and something or someone touched me on the leg and woke me up. As I opened my eyes I saw two eyes staring into mine . . . looking right at me in the dark.

"After that he became a regular terror—not doing anything malicious, you understand, but just making his presence known so frequently that it kept all of us constantly on edge. He stomped around the house at will. Sometimes he bumped a hanging lamp and it wriggled in his wake. Sometimes he slammed a door or moved a chair or made funny noises. But most often he stayed cooped up in the attic."

This attic room, located beneath the eaves of the house, is only fifteen feet by nine feet in size, and it is a hotbox. It has two windows, but they do little to cool things off. The window on the north still has the original casing on it, and has been nailed shut to keep it from falling out and getting broken. The other window, on the front of the house, only opens from the top. Mrs. Cook said, "My husband fixed it that way when our children were small to keep them from falling out of it."

This house was built sometime toward the end of the last century. After it was finished, it was apparently discovered that more room was needed; and so the little attic room was added. There was no possible place to put a stairway, however. So in order to get in and out of this room you have to crawl through a hole in the floor that is five feet long and three feet wide. The steep but sturdy ladder down which you climb ends up in the bathroom.

Adjoining the attic room is the furnace room—one more peculiar thing about this house, for the gas-forced air furnace has been installed there, in an almost inaccessible area. In order to get to it you have to hold onto a rope suspended from the rafters and crawl through a hole some thirty inches square and thirty-nine inches up from the floor, in the side of the wall. The furnace had to be put up there in the unused space of the attic, Mrs. Cook explained, because there is no basement to their house and each room has a foundation on solid rock.

I am going into some detail about this queer furnace room and its absurd entrance because it figures in a later episode that must have nearly frightened Mrs. Cook out of her skull.

After she began to hear things herself in her house, and especially after she saw those eyes, Faye began to conjecture about why she would have a ghost in her attic. She determined to ask around in the neighborhood to learn if there had been an unusual death in the house. She did not have far to go. Her next-door neighbors had lived there a long time, and so they knew the answer to her question. A man had committed suicide in the house, hanging himself from the attic down through the ladder opening.

Now that she had something to go on, the thing Faye felt she must do was to learn what she could from the entity himself, and to try to help him if possible.

Faye Cook is the kind of person who feels an obligation to spend her time and efforts for other people when they need her. Her yard is a perfect illustration of the efforts she has made for the children of her neighborhood. It has a little shrine to St. Francis of Assisi. She told me, "Perhaps you think it's strange for a Mormon to have a Catholic symbol in her yard. To me, St. Francis is not merely a saint of the Catholic Church, but a symbol of love and devotion to God. I have always been fascinated by legends and I use a lot of legends in my poetry and short stories. A long time ago, I heard the legend of St. Francis of Assisi and of how the birds and animals sought refuge from the huntsmen beneath the folds of his robes."

Being also a lover of animals, she decided she should have a statue of St. Francis for her garden, and she searched until she found one. Delighted, she placed it in the yard, surrounded by miniature animals. Now it has grown into a playground for fairies, elves, Pinocchio, Bambi, and all the little figures she has been able to find to represent stories of interest to children.

Faye wrote one of her favorite stories, titled "The Fairest of the Fairies at the Fair," for a little blind boy in the neighborhood. She wanted to help him to learn, and also to get him acquainted with the other nearby children. "When the others saw him with me out in the yard," she said, "they would gather here and I'd tell them stories and read them poems. The little blind boy had just enough sight to see about three inches away and no farther. He was considered noneducable, but after I got him interested in learning, then a visiting teacher began to come twice a week and give him lessons. He had learned the entire first reader by the time they moved away from here. He was not as hopeless as many people thought."

Mrs. Cook had such a sweet smile as she talked about the children. "If I ever make any money from my poetry," she said, "I'm going to use at least part of it to put some child through college. In this way I can repay God for permitting me to write these poems and stories."

It is no wonder that such a woman decided to try to give aid to some poor lost entity who may be wandering around her house unseen. "One day I asked the ghost if he would give me his name so that I could know what to call him," she told me. "Then I began to hear sounds coming from the furnace that somehow answered the question for me. We'd had our furnace installed at just that time, but it had not made strange noises before, nor has it done so since. But that day sounds came through the vent in my bedroom. I was sitting there trying to relax for a while before I went to babysit for my daughter. The sounds were almost musical—like just one instrument of some kind playing. Since I had asked the ghost his name, I attempted to interpret what I was hearing as an answer to my question. I decided that perhaps one of these musical notes sounded as if it were played on an oboe, so I hit upon the name 'Obie.' Then

came a deeper note, more as if it were played on a tuba. So I
put the two words together and felt certain that the name I was
trying to get was 'Toby.'

"We had bought this house from a man name James Gibbs
who told us it had been built by his father," Faye went on. "And
so I naturally concluded that my Toby was named Tobias Gibbs.
He has since confirmed this."

When people who get psychic impressions and accept uncriti-
cally what they receive report specific events like the reception
of a name, it would be especially nice if they would turn out to
be provable. But somehow they rarely are. There appear to be
no records that a man named Tobias Gibbs committed suicide in
that house or neighborhood. And yet we have to remember that
records about such things were considerably more casual in the
last century. Mrs. Cook is sincere and she is convinced, and she
believes she has a certain amount of evidence about Toby's apparent suicide because the same thing nearly happened to her.

Now, how did Tom Carlin get into this act—he of the "poison-
pen letter"? It came about in this manner: In 1967, while chat-
ting on his radio program about ghosts, "Talktician" Tom had
some calls in response asking if he would conduct a haunted-
house tour in the Salt Lake area. He replied that he would if
he received enough postcards about it to warrant such a tour
. . . and provided he could find an authentic haunted house. The
station was flooded with postcards, proving, as I have long
maintained, that many more persons are interested in ghosts
than is ordinarily believed. After receiving over a thousand
cards, Tom called a halt. He had in the meantime learned about
three haunted houses. One of these burned to the ground before
an expedition to investigate it could be arranged. Real estate
agents, as real estate agents are wont, refused to allow permission to visit the other two. So there was the announcer and a
thousand listeners all eager and avid for a ghost hunt—and no
object of their attention available.

A woman (Kay Christiansen) who said she was a spiritual

sensitive was being interviewed in May 1967 and she asked anyone interested in extrasensory perception to call her. Faye Cook phoned her to ask what to do about Tobias Gibbs. Faye says, "We discussed the strange things that had been happening in this house. She told me that I might have an earthbound spirit here, and I was fairly sure she was right. Yet, there are always doubts in one's mind. So, when they asked, I decided to go ahead and let Tom Carlin bring some people here to investigate this house. I thought they might be able to determine if there was a real ghost here or if I was imagining all these things."

Toby was warned in advance of their coming. He responded with a poem. I asked Mrs. Cook how she received it. Could she hear Toby?

"In a way," she said. "It came to me as if someone were whispering in my ear. Over and over the same words came, so I decided to write them down. When I saw what it was I showed it to Tom and the rest who visited me."

Here is the poem by a purported spirit named Tobias Gibbs via the mediumship of Faye Cook.

> When they come here, I will not show
>   My face to them, because I know
> They may have come here just to laugh
>   Or try to get my photograph.
>
> I'll talk to them, this much I'll do
>   But I'll just show my face to you.
> I may send others in my place
>   But only you may see my face.

I wondered what he meant about "only you may see my face" because until that time Mrs. Cook had not told me anything about having *seen* her ghost. She had not, at the time the poem was written, she told me. Since then she has seen him twice. The first sighting was on May 7, 1968. By then she had decided it was necessary to practice exorcism rites to rid her house of spirits. Having Toby around was not so bad, but she was not sure but what he had begun to bring in a certain element of rowdy accomplices. She realized that some of the things she had been lending her unwitting support to were against her Mormon religion, and so she decided the time had come to take steps.

"As I shut my eyes that night," she told me, "I saw two figures dressed in white standing beside a young man who looked about twenty years old. This was undoubtedly my Toby. The spirits were talking to him and telling him that he must go with them and leave the house alone." Apparently he acquiesced, at least temporarily, for things were quiet around there for some time. Yet in October of the same year she saw this identical young man sitting on her bed. "I asked him why he had not gone with them and he said, 'My work here is not finished.' What he meant by that I did not then know, but now I do. Later he warned me of danger, and I now suspect that if it were not for him this story of my experiences would have ended abruptly before it began."

The report of how he alerted her to her peril, or protected her from it, will follow in due time. We have not yet completed the account of the séance of July 10, 1967. That was the date chosen by Tom Carlin and his group to visit the Cook residence. The radio personality wears a beard and moustache and has a definitely theatrical appearance and air about him, perhaps because he is very active in Little Theater. He was also, at the time he made this visit, a man very skeptical of ghosts.

Of all those listeners to his program who had expressed a desire to go along on the expedition, Carlin had selected eleven. They included Mrs. Christiansen and Douglas MacGregor, a veteran haunted-house investigator who is a chemist working for a Ph.D. in science at the University of Utah. The rest of the group were university undergraduates.

MacGregor took along instruments to measure vapors, temperature changes, vibrations, and charges of electricity. During the evening they revealed no dramatic temperature changes and no presence of electricity where it should not have been. Nonetheless, most of those participating in the séance insisted that they felt cold winds blowing on them.

The temperature had risen to 110 degrees that day in the Salt Lake Valley. Inside the little attic room where they were all crowded on chairs and the floor it was as hot and cozy as the nest of a setting hen. No draft was coming in through that one partially open window. and yet, later on, several of the visitors said they felt cold air touch their faces and necks. Tom Carlin was one of them. He had a number of strange sensations inside that room, and his skepticism melted fast—as well as his collar. He later said, "I was plenty doubtful about the ghost story; but then I felt the cold touch me. And I distinctly smelled the odor of bay rum which I remember from my childhood. This matched the story of the man who died in the attic a quarter of a century ago. He reportedly drank bay rum." (That could not have been Toby, who died at the turn of the century, some sixty-seven years before. I asked Tom where he got this information, but I never did get a clear answer. Maybe he was talking about ghosts in general, who can easily be reported to have been addicted to bay rum or alcohol, shoe polish, glue or soap bubbles, and no one can refute it.)

It was still faintly light as the séance began. In that area it does not get really dark until about ten o'clock at night during the summer. In the twilight MacGregor set up his equipment on the north side of the room. He handed Tom and several others packages of Polaroid film, factory wrapped, lead-foil covered, and tightly sealed. Carlin laid his pack of film on the floor and said he was going to sit on it all during the meeting.

Right away one of the youths, named Don, went into a trance (or at least, he appeared to). Of course it is possible that he was putting this on; but it is also possible that he was a natural medium and went into the trance inadvertently. I have seen this happen on occasion at séances. It is also usual for one or two persons to go to sleep because they are sitting quietly in the dark and just cannot stay awake. The rule for this is—if he snores, wake him up.

Giving Don the benefit of the doubt, if he were in a genuine trance he was not the host to a very amiable spirit. It was about then that some persons in the room began to get exceedingly cold. It was not, as Mrs. Cook pointed out, "the ordinary kind of cold that you experience when you go out in the winter, but a clammy cold." Then Don, in his apparently entranced state, started raving and shouting. He called the others unpleasant names and told them to get the hell out of the room. Kay Christiansen asked who was talking through him and he replied, "Uncle Marvin."

"Why are you here?" Kay asked.

"To scare the hell out of you," he replied. And he just about did, from all reports.

After the group had more conversation with Uncle Marvin, Don came out of his trance; but almost as soon as his eyes were open another youth, Kim, started shouting, "No, you can't be here, you're dead, you can't be here." He began to shake all over. Kay, who was having to play den mother to the whole crowd, went over and sat on the north side of him to keep him from falling down the hole in the floor where the ladder was. Kim quieted down after Kay sat beside him. She asked him what was going on and he described an experience romping across a meadow with his deceased grandmother. This was particularly impressive to him because she had been crippled with arthritis and her legs had become paralyzed shortly before she died. Kay let Kim have his visit with his grandmother for a while and then woke him up. After that very little more occurred, and soon the séance was over.

Doug MacGregor, when I consulted him about that evening's experience, was inclined to dismiss the trances as either farce or fantasy. He also thought those who had felt the cold drafts and smelled the bay rum were just susceptible to suggestion—after all, *he* had not felt any cold or smelled anything unusual. And the apparatus he had brought recorded nothing unusual.

MacGregor has investigated a haunted house in Watsonville, California, for the American Society for Psychical Research. He knows how to organize ghost hunts and he has observed some definite poltergeist phenomena. He told me that in Watsonville he had been able to photograph objects in flight and other poltergeist activity during the actual time it was going on. He was not impressed by the proceedings that night in Murray, Utah. This was because he'd had no control over conditions.

MacGregor did feel fairly secure in the test he had prepared with the film, however. He had brought Polaroid films for a four-by-five professional press camera, each one of which is packaged separately. Had the foil cover been opened or tampered with in any way it would have been obvious. Nonetheless, it might have been possible for someone to make some kind of an impression on the film by pressure on the outside of the package, had an opportunity been given to do so in advance. In this instance, he had brought the film himself and no one else knew about it beforehand; and there did not seem to have been a chance for anyone in the group to have tampered with the film during the evening. Tom Carlin insisted he was sitting on his all evening. And he should know.

So what was the only manifestation that came out of the evening's séance? The thing that put the cold chills down Tom's back as well as around his neck and ears? It was the "poison-pen letter"!

Picture this scene. The whole crowd has left the attic at the end of the meeting and now they are all assembled in the bathroom at the foot of the ladder. Doug MacGregor examines each package of film as carefully as possible in the dim light in the bathroom. No scratches or dents are observable on them. Then he opens each in turn. Nothing on the first one . . . nothing on the second one . . . but on the one Tom Carlin sat on was a crudely but sharply etched message in childish printing: DANGER!

Tom has refused ever to go back into that attic room again. "Let's just say I'm cautious," he said. "Let whoever is there stay there and I'll stay here. When the roll is called up yonder, we can get together and discuss it."

After hearing Tom Carlin and the others hash and rehash the events at the famous haunted house in Murray, the rest of the staff of Radio Station KSXX decided to see for themselves what was going on. They asked for permission to investigate the house, and, Mrs. Cook says, "Having nothing to hide, I invited them out here." So on November 10, 1967, a group from the station arrived, accompanied by Kay Christiansen, who was in charge as Tom Carlin's deputy. Tom suddenly had some very pressing business elsewhere. "I know where I'm not wanted," he said.

Nothing much of interest occurred on this night, nor has much happened on subsequent nights when séances have been attempted there. Perhaps Toby was getting bored being investigated. He laid so low that Mrs. Cook almost thought he had left the place, until . . .

"Until November 15, 1968," said Faye. "On that night I awoke to the same touch on my leg that had started all this in the first place, and then I saw the eyes again . . . staring into mine. I was not afraid of Toby now, and I stared right back. But as I did so I began to have a vision—I could see my son lying by his car, bleeding from many cuts. This picture stayed in my mind and I was terribly worried about what it could mean.

"The next day my son Gordan and his wife Mary, who live in Salt Lake City, came by with their baby son, Donald. They left here about 1:30 and, do you know, when they went I had a distinct urge to go home with them. Perhaps if I had been with them the accident would not have happened. But it did. They were in a smashup with another car and all of them severely injured, Gordan and the baby suffering skull fractures and Mary, a concussion. Fortunately, they all improved steadily."

Faye does not think for one moment that the ghost caused this accident. Certainly not. She does suspect that with his supernormal foreknowledge of events he tried to alert her, perhaps so that she could somehow avert its occurrence. Toby certainly proved to be a help in the next episode; she feels no possible doubt about that.

That odd furnace room at the Cook house is also used for storage. On December 1, 1968, Faye crawled through the hole to get out some Christmas ornaments and check them over. She had stepped onto a folding chair in order to climb through the hole in the wall, and now as she stepped back down on it, the chair started to fold up. She told me, "I heard a voice speaking to me as plain as day saying, 'Go with the chair!' My instinct was to try to jump off it, but had I done so I could have killed myself, for I would surely have fallen down that big hole in the floor where the ladder is. As it was, by throwing my weight back toward the chair, my feet got tangled up in it; but it seemed as if the chair was moving away from the hole. I fell to the floor —but not down the hole!

"After my nerves calmed down, I heard this same voice speaking again. 'That is how I died,' it said. I have been able to put the puzzle together, and now I think I know how Toby really killed himself. He had tied a rope to the rafters in what is now our furnace room and kept the other end of it out in the attic room. There was a noose on the end of the rope for him to put his foot in when he came down out of the storage room. He had some object to stand on to raise himself high enough to reach the hole in the wall. He got in there all right, but when he started to come out the thing he put his foot on slipped and he fell. As he did so his head went into the noose, his body fell down through the hole in the floor, and there he was—hanging down the ladder. Those who found him believed he had committed suicide; I even believed it at first, but now I know that he died accidentally. Perhaps now that the true story about what happened here in this house is being published the spirit of Tobias Gibbs can rest."

"But what," I asked her, "if you need him again, to warn you of danger or tell you how to avoid it?"

"I'll just have to take my chances. I got along all right without him before I moved in here. I don't think one should get too dependent on anyone else, even a ghost."

CHAPTER XI

Fort Sam Houston's Harvey

"A GHOST doesn't have a throat. How could I possibly hear a ghost clearing its throat?" Margaret Green asked herself. But if it was not a ghost, what was it? There was no one else in the huge, empty, lonely Service Club No. 2 in the U.S. Army Medical Training Center at Fort Sam Houston, Texas. It is always closed up tight until noon. Mrs. Green, the program director, had entered the building with her key and was sure she was the first person to arrive. No one else was even due for a while. Nonetheless, as she was putting her evening's lunch in the refrigerator, she heard someone "harrumph" right behind her. She began to dash about all over the building to discover who did it. By the time she had reconnoitered thoroughly she was convinced she was alone there. Now she had to account for that cleared throat some other way.

There is no mechanical noise in the Service Club that sounds like a harrumph. As Manuel Ortiz, the maintenance engineer, points out, when you work around a building as much as the staff has worked there, you learn all the sounds that are native to it. You know all its little plumbing noises and its furnace noises and its pipe noises. You also know all the creaks and groans of its settlings and saggings.

Thus when someone cleared his throat right in the room with her, and no one was there, Mrs. Green knew it was no ordinary building sound. She still would not have been inclined to attribute it to a ghost if it had not been that "Harvey" was already well-known around there. No invisible rabbit, he is credited with being an unseen man, possibly the one who committed suicide in that building about eighteen years before. Once you begin to include a spook in your reckoning of events, it becomes easy to give a ghostly interpretation to everything. That is why most of the personnel at this Army Service Club always assure themselves of every opportunity to find a normal means of explanation first for their unusual phenomena. They bend over backwards to be objective, but usually end up acknowledging Harvey anyway, because so much goes on around there that is completely inexplicable.

Harvey has never caused any real grief. He is not malicious, but he has definitely been making his presence known for some years. Service Club Director Phyllis Boyes thinks he has a goal in life—or should I say afterlife? She thinks he wants to cause enough uproar to get the wheels turning for a new, larger, and better-equipped facility. If you have to put up with a ghost in your line of work, as Miss Boyes does, you might as well adopt a positive approach to it and attribute its interest in the place to some worthy cause.

Certainly Harvey is no figment of any highpowered imaginations. He has made his presence known to too many people for that. There was a period of time in 1967–68 when he became quite a nuisance opening windows after they had been carefully locked for the night. Let us consider the testimony of several of those who have been inconvenienced in this manner.

"In the first place," Miss Boyes told me, "when a building is left open here at the installation it means that the Military Police call you whenever they discover it, no matter what time of night. You then have to return to the building to check it out and make sure there hasn't been a break-in. This, at some unpleasant hour like two o'clock in the morning, can be a bit irritating. So closing up the place and securing it is very important. This is why I got so put out with the young men to whom I entrusted this job. They assured me that they had carefully locked up in each case, but as we would leave the building we would look back and see a window open. This happened time and time again and I insisted the men were being very careless. Finally we set up a system where one fellow would close up the building and then two of us would go around checking on him. We would then leave, vowing that all the windows and doors were thoroughly locked. We might still, as like as not, find an upstairs window open when we looked back."

Phyllis Boyes mentioned this to her supervisor, Ardyce Pfanstiel, because she did not want her to think she was being completely careless in the security of the club. She told Miss Pfanstiel, "You know, we have some really weird things going on," and she explained about the windows. She ended up with, "I think this place is real spooky."

Miss Boyes did not suspect she was going to strike such a responsive chord, but Miss Pfanstiel's reply was, "You are not just kidding." She, it was then revealed, had undergone similar experiences when she was there as Service Club Director as long ago as 1960.

Perhaps the purpose and activity of Service Clubs should be mentioned. They are in a way like USO's except that USO's operate off post and the Service Clubs operate on post—at all U.S. military installations. Fort Sam Houston was established in 1876 and was the birthplace of the Army Air Corps. It was for a great many years the largest Army Post in the country, but now it has become a medical training center. Service Clubs are open to all enlisted personnel and members of their families; but because of its location in the middle of the troop area of the Medical Training Center, 99.9 per cent of the men who patronize Club

No. 2 are trainees. The Medical Training Center is the only place in the United States that trains combat medics and the medical aidmen who are of such value in all war areas and dispensaries. When these trainees are off duty they need recreation, and the Army Service Club program furnishes the place for it, with suitable supplies and equipment. It is staffed by uniformed civilian Service Club director personnel. These workers try to provide the soldiers "a home away from home" with friendly and wholesome social and recreational activities, an informal community hangout as well as a professionally run and equipped recreation center.

In any week Special Service Club No. 2 might have Ping-Pong, card, and pool tournaments, coffeehouses, plays, talent contests, charades and other games, birthday parties, slide shows, or any number of other group activities. Also available are rooms where trainees who so desire may privately play records, write letters, or practice on any of a number of musical instruments. Dances are usually held at Service Clubs, but No. 2 has too small an auditorium for them. Since approximately 25,000 enlisted men are entertained every month there, it is difficult to find space for much that the directors would like to provide for them. That is where Harvey comes in. Is he really trying to scare the club out of the building and into larger quarters? Let us see what he has been up to there.

Mrs. Green, who heard the "harrumph," is, Miss Boyes assured me, a woman not given to wild imaginings. If she said she heard someone clearing his voice, that is what she heard. "Now *I* can imagine things," Miss Boyes emphasized. "I have to watch myself to make sure that it is not my imagination playing tricks on me when something occurs; but Mrs. Green, who is now retired, did not ordinarily have that problem." That is why when Mrs. Green said she *heard* Harvey, Phyllis Boyes is sure she did. She also *saw* a number of windows open after they had been securely locked.

I was shown these windows, which have self-locking devices

that fasten securely when they are closed. I had wondered if they might be able to slip up and down by themselves due to a faulty sash, but was shown the bolts on each that slip into holes in the frame so securely that the windows cannot possibly go up unless someone releases the bolts deliberately. Neither can they be broken into from the outside without shattering the glass.

First Sgt. Louis Milligan, who works the evening shift from six to ten o'clock, told me about the first time he discovered that the windows do not stay shut when the ghost cares to open them. Louis said, "I had closed all the windows—we go around with a flashlight checking each of them—and then as I left the building the one right over the front door was wide open."

"Mrs. Green," Louis yelled, "the window upstairs is open!"

"I just checked behind you and it was locked," Mrs. Green replied.

"Well, it's open now." So both of them went back upstairs to close it. No one was there, of course. No one but invisible Harvey.

They next incident Sgt. Milligan recalls occurred when he came on duty on a Sunday afternoon and was jumped on because the windows had been left open again the night before.

"I think I'm going crazy," Milligan said, "because I could swear that I locked those windows." So on this Sunday night he and the other workers decided to double-check each other. "As I locked the windows another of the fellows came behind me and tested to make sure they were locked correctly. Then we came downstairs and as we were getting ready to leave we walked out the door and looked up and the window in that same music room over the front door was open. Three people had checked that window, including Mrs. Green, the program director."

Sgt. Milligan, a Negro who has made himself so indispensable to the Service Club that there are almost tears when he goes on vacation, told me that the "crowning glory of the whole thing" occurred the night "we were closing up and Ben Paniagua and I were by ourselves. We had fastened up everything securely and were getting ready to leave. Then just as we were in the lobby we heard this beautiful music. It seemed to be coming out of the ceiling. We were waiting for the Officer of the Day to come and check the club before we left. I didn't say anything about the music to Ben and he didn't say anything to me at first. I did not want him to think I was cracking up and I guess he felt the same way. But finally he said, 'Do you hear what I hear?' I said, 'Yes, music coming out of the ceiling.' Then the O.D. walked in and we said, 'Do you hear what we hear?' He said, 'Music coming out of the ceiling.' 'Yes,' we said, 'and there's nobody up there.' So I went to the crest of the stairwell and looked, but there was definitely nobody up there. It sounded like beautiful music, probably a flute. I didn't recognize it, but it was sweet . . . a tune, but an unidentifiable one."

Ben Paniagua, a civilian recreation aid in Special Services, independently confirmed what Milligan had said. A handsome, dimpled young Mexican who attends San Antonio College in the daytime and works at the Service Club in the evening, Ben told me a similar tale. He said, "First Louis Milligan and I had closed up. It was around the time of Hurricane Beulah—September 20–23, 1967. We were waiting in the lobby and all of a sudden we heard music like a flute. It was not very coordinated, but it sounded something like a tune. Sometimes I noticed it sounded flat. Milligan decided it was upstairs and he started walking up the steps and it stopped. It started again when he came down. Then the O.D., Capt. Anderson, came in. He is now a Major. He heard it too."

Phyllis Boyes was on vacation at the time this occurred. She says, "When I returned no one said 'hello' or anything else except, 'Guess what! Harvey's back and now he's musical.' "

Certainly the staff tried to learn if there was a natural cause for this unauthorized music. Was a radio left on? Had some mechanical device in the building begun to pick up musical sounds from the air as sometimes may occur? They investigated, Miss Boyes told me, "to see if an AWOL was hiding out in the attic."

Maintenance engineers were called in to check all the vents and openings in case someone might be concealing himself there. Phyllis even put masking tape on all the exits from the attic so that if anyone were up there he would have to break the tape to come down; but the tape was never broken.

All these people involved with the Fort Sam Houston haunt are droll when they tell about its antics. Nothing has occurred to frighten them or really disturb anything except their sense of what is normal in this world. Many questions are asked, all the staff members are critical of what they see and hear, yet they are highly entertained by it. They are all well-trained career people who have their wits about them and have been in their professions for a long time. Miss Boyes, for instance, told me she had started in her work by running cafeterias in Army Service Clubs in World War II. "I served coffee and doughnuts in Europe to front-line troops for the Red Cross," she said. "I have a Bronze Star—for service, not bravery." After the war she worked in Japan, and Panama, and then spent seven happy years in Hawaii. Now enjoying her stay at Fort Sam Houston, she hopes to remain there, at least until she gets Harvey straightened out.

Ben Paniagua told me of another occasion shortly after the music episode, when he and Louis Milligan were in the check-out room where they keep the musical instruments. They were making sure each instrument had been returned to its shelf and were closing the doors of the cabinets. Their backs were turned to the only typewriter in the room when suddenly they heard the sound of the carriage moving across the machine abruptly enough to cause the bell to ring. "We turned around," Ben said, "but there was no one anywhere in the room, or the building, for that matter. After that we practiced a number of times trying to make the carriage of the typewriter throw itself across automatically and cause that noise; but it was impossible."

Louis Milligan independently confirmed Paniagua's account of this. He added that neither of them were close enough to the machine to have flipped the carriage as a joke on the other. They

were both standing side by side with their backs to the typewriter.

Milligan mentioned another incident which occurred when a
young soldier named Billy Gray was helping out around there
as a volunteer. "We had told him about the ghost but he hàd
refused to accept our tales as anything except our own alibis for
goofing off or something. One night as we were closing up we
had been talking about Harvey. As he walked upstairs Billy said
out loud, 'Harvey, if you're up here you gotta make me *know* it.'
A few minutes later we heard a door slam. It sounded to us
downstairs just like a screen door. To Billy, who was in the record room, it sounded like the record room door had slammed.
Only thing was, the actual door had not moved and did not
close. But Billy heard it slam right beside him. He came downstairs white as a sheet and he was a believer. He never made
fun of us again."

Louis is a first sergeant in the Inflatable Mobile Surgical Hospital, known as MUST—Medical Unit Selfcontained Transporta-
ble. "We call it the Balloon Platoon," he said. "It's the newest
thing in the U.S. Army." The sergeant has been in the Army for
twenty-two years, having served in Korea, Okinawa, and Japan,
and traveled all over the world except Russia. His favorite program at the Service Club is what they call Mad Art, a class in
far-out and imaginative painting. He showed me some beautiful
and original art work his pupils had done, even though he makes
light of the class, saying, "You don't have to be an artist to get in
but you do have to be a bit mad."

Asked for more of his experiences with the ghost, Milligan
said, "One afternoon I was here in the office, and Mrs. Green
was at her desk and there was no one else in the club. We were
sitting talking about the program when all of a sudden we heard
footsteps going across the floor above us. You know the crunch,
crunch, crunch. Mrs. Green said, 'Oh, there's someone upstairs!'
I started up the stairway quietly and tiptoed to the place where
we had heard the steps. If you go up the way I did there is no

possible chance that anyone could get by you. They would either have to pass you or go down the fire escape. No one came by me, and no one went out the door to the fire escape because it was locked from the inside. Even the screen door was hooked. I checked each room upstairs carefully and there was no one anywhere.

"I got back downstairs and told Mrs. Green, 'There's no one there.' After I sat down the footsteps started up again. We just gave up, because what else could we do? We said, 'There's Harvey again.' "

The sergeant added, "I thought once I'd taken Harvey home with me because of what happened with my electric saw. I was doing some work at home one Saturday and decided to use it, but when I looked for it I couldn't find it. My wife, Fannie, and I searched for it all over the house but it was not there. I worked Sunday and forgot about it. Monday when I got to my office here on Fort Sam Houston my electric saw was under my desk. I don't know from that day to this how that saw got there."

"Where do you live?" I asked him.

"I live off post but nearby," said Louis.

"Had you ever brought the saw from home?"

"Never." He was emphatic.

"Did the saw belong to you, personally?"

"It was my saw in my case with my name on it . . . and it was under my desk. I hadn't loaned it to anyone. Nobody could have stolen or borrowed it without either my wife or myself knowing it. I just can't find any possible way to account for it. My wife knew I had not taken it away from home. I knew I had not brought it to the office. Such a thing worries you. You wonder if you might have blacked out or something. It's frightening."

Manuel Ortiz, the maintenance engineer mentioned earlier, is responsible for two good stories. One involved the latches on the windows of the pool room. These have to be especially checked, for they do not lock automatically as the other windows do. They have those little levers at the top that we are familiar with on most old-style windows. Sometimes these catches can be cranky, and one night Margaret Green had trouble with them; but finally she got all the windows in the pool room locked. She particularly asked Ortiz to test them after her, because of her difficulty. He did, and they were all fastened. Yet when the O.D. came in to check, he raised the windows with no effort. They were not locked then.

On another occasion Ortiz was repairing the air conditioner in the auditorium one morning and he heard someone walking upstairs. He knew that no one was supposed to be up there at that hour, so he chased up the steps to see who it was. He looked into every room, but no one was there. When he returned to the first floor and continued his work he began to hear the sounds of several people walking up and down the hallway upstairs. Miss Boyes says, "Ortiz has announced that he will not come back into this building unless one of us is here. He doesn't care a thing for Harvey."

One tends to conjecture about the accounts of a ghost in a place like this. There is obviously something unusual going on, but what is it and why? A story like the last one, "Only You May See My Face," does not have to be taken seriously. Although the possibility exists that it might be the account of the activities of a real ghost, it might just as easily represent merely the wishful thinking of a sensitive woman and the desire for excitement on the part of a public figure. The case of Harvey, however, produces convincing testimony from a variety of responsible people, all of whom have experienced similar supernormal manifestations here.

We go to our list of definitions of ghosts without too much success in classifying this activity. The sounds of footsteps, music, and harrumphs could possibly be explained as "memory images" repeating themselves over and over again, except that the music and the harrumph only occurred once. This concept is also refuted by the raised windows, which gives evidence of something actively engaged in physical manifestations. Could it truly be the spirit of that unhappy man who hanged himself there long ago? If so, what is he up to? It might be mischief, but it is certainly not malice. Because he seems to have ill will toward no one, what reason for his efforts is any more realistic than Miss Boyes's pretense that he still hangs around in order to do the club a good turn?

Miss Ardyce Pfanstiel, who is now the Service Club supervisor at Fort Sam Houston, researched the history of the building for me to discover what she could about the chap who committed suicide there; but only the fact of his violent self-inflicted death was on record. No data about him were available. The Service Club No. 2 edifice was constructed in 1946 for hospital recreation and staffed by the American Red Cross. Later it was used as a Red Cross guest house. In 1951 it was converted to a headquarters building for the Medical Training Center. It was at that time that the young man hanged himself from the pipes in what is now called the Chair Room, a small storage area just off the auditorium where additional chairs are stacked and stored.

Miss Pfanstiel has several stories to tell about what happened ghostwise when she was the director at Club No. 2. She has reservations about the first instance, however. "It could possibly have been my imagination," she said, "so I have tended to discount it. I was in a situation where my fancy might have affected my powers of observation, although I don't feel that it did. I forgot my purse one night and had to go back into the empty club to retrieve it. Now, when this building is closed it is more silent, ominous, and depressing than you can imagine."

I *could* imagine, and I told her so. That very afternoon I had discerned how impregnable and lonesome-looking it was when I had tried to get into it to keep my appointment with Miss Pfanstiel and Miss Boyes. Service Club No. 2 is a big barracks-like structure of hollow-cement-block construction about fifteen to sixteen thousand square feet in area. There are seven entrances, all of which are kept locked during the hours when the

club is not open to the enlisted men, no matter how many of the
staff members are working inside. Carrying my heavy case containing camera and tape recorder, I trudged completely around
the building, trying each door and discovering it to be locked. It
looked just like a deserted school the day after summer vacation
starts, and I could not believe anyone was inside. Yet I was sure
I had come to the right place; and after all the trouble I'd had
locating it in the vast maze of Fort Sam Houston I felt slightly
miffed at its deserted-and-forgotten appearance. Naturally as-
suming that when all the entrances were securely locked it was
not meant to be invaded, I did not stand and pound on any of
the doors; but I should have. An M.P. to whom I eventually appealed for help did that, and he got results promptly.

Well, Miss Pfanstiel had the same lonely reaction at eleven
o'clock at night when she had to make her way around the dark
building to the east door to use her key and enter. When she
walked in everything was pitch dark except for one small ray of
illumination coming from the front hall. She turned on the lights
and walked over to her desk.

"Then," she said, "as I pulled out the drawer to get my purse
I very distinctly heard someone playing Ping-Pong. It went
'ping,' 'pong,' 'ping,' 'pong.' Needless to say I got the hell out of
this building. No one else was in there, but *someone* was playing
Ping-Pong."

That is a sad idea. I do not like to think of Harvey in there
alone playing Ping-Pong by himself. I would rather conjecture
some charming female spirit companion who joins him at night
for fun and games.

Miss Pfanstiel went on: "The second instance, which was even
more eerie, happened on November 5, 1960. Prior to this date
we'd had a full month of programing leading up to the national
presidential elections—with various trainees competing against
each other for the title of "Citizen Soldier." The entire clubhouse
was decorated in the decor of the traditional elephant and donkey. Right in the center of the auditorium, hanging from the

rafters high up in the ceiling, we had two piñatas, an elephant and a donkey."

Piñatas are known in Mexico and Texas for the roles they play at parties. Now primarily made of papier-mâché or tissue paper, they are used for decoration. Originally they were made of pottery and held gifts or sweets. A large clay figure of some object with significance for the time of year, the piñata was hung in the center of the room at parties in Mexico. When time came to distribute the goodies it contained, the children hit at it with sticks until they broke it and its contents spilled into eager hands. Today the forms the decorative piñatas take are such things as Easter bunnies, dolls, eggs, Santa Clauses, donkeys, and elephants.

After the club was closed on the final night of the election campaign, the auditorium was dark. The overhead lights and the ventilating system had been turned off and the staff was closing up for the night. Except for a yawn or two and a few tired goodnights, the silence was overwhelming. Then there was a soft, dull thud. Miss Pfanstiel says, "My program director, Corinne Eadie, and I looked at each other questioningly and headed for the auditorium. On the floor was one of the papier-mâché piñata figures. I picked it up and then we stared toward the ceiling where the second piñata was moving rapidly back and forth. There was no wind, no breath of air, for the ventilating system, as I have said, was turned off. The auditorium was even stuffy. But there was the figure swinging gaily—and it was the donkey!

"Miss Eadie said, 'I wonder if that is a prediction of things to come.' It was, of course—for the Democrats were elected."

I asked Ardyce Pfanstiel if the two piñatas had been tied together, so that if one broke loose and fell by chance it could set the other in motion. She assured me that they had been suspended from the rafters separately about four or five feet apart. The swish of air from the one descending could hardly have caused even slight movement by the other.

"Yet," said Miss Pfanstiel, "that jackass was swinging back and forth quite violently. We decided that if anyone were still around there invisibly, he was trying to give us a message—a prediction of the outcome of the election."

One could almost suspect that this ghost was invented for the purpose of drawing attention to the need of a larger service club, as they laughingly suggested, except that all the people I talked to about Harvey are such sincere and obviously critical people. Also, I was not approached with the story initially. It came to me in a very roundabout way from someone who had merely heard rumors of the Fort Sam Houston haunt.

Miss Pfanstiel and Miss Boyes are both goodnatured, attractive, gregarious, and intelligent women. They may enjoy their ghost, and tease about Harvey's efforts to get them more space for Service Club No. 2, but they are positive in their realization for the need of a larger facility.

"This club is inadequate in many ways," Miss Boyes declared. "Dances are out because the auditorium is too small. There is not a soundproofed room in the building. If we have a play or show in progress in the auditorium no one else can play records or practice music anywhere. I don't like the feeling that I am grabbing them by the neck and saying, 'Tonight you *will* watch a show,' but that seems to be what I have to do. We have all kinds of things for the men to do on their own if they prefer to (we call it our 'do-it-yourself kit'); but if something is being presented in the auditorium we have to keep the rest of the building quiet. Even a record player upstairs can be heard in the auditorium. We need soundproofing in the record rooms and writing rooms."

Miss Boyes sighed. "The average civilian does not have any idea of the concern a Service Club director has for the young soldier or airman who uses her facility," she said. "We really feel it when we are unable to provide as much wholesome recreation for them as we would like."

"Because you are No. 2 you've got to try harder," I told her.

"Oh, we do, we do," she assured me. "And that's where Harvey should come in. If a ghost is going to be of any value to a place he's got to cause a lot of commotion. Up to now Harvey has not been able to scare us out of here and if he can't do that I don't know what else he's good for."

If anything happens that Service Club No. 2 gets tired of Harvey, they can always pass him along. Miss Boyes said, "I mentioned to one of our chaplains that I had given Harvey the responsibility of getting us a much-needed new Service Club.

"He said, 'Well, if it works may I borrow him? We need a new chapel.'"

CHAPTER XII

Murders in Maine

ON THE LAST LAP of my trip around the United States in 1966 when I was doing research for *Prominent American Ghosts,* I covered New England, not suspecting that I would there have the fright of my life. On Friday, July 1, I left New York City for Albany, where I met my friend Leah Exon of New York and Naples, Italy. She accompanied me for the first part of the New England trip, but we detoured over the Fourth of July holiday to visit mutual friends in Canada.

We drove first to Montreal, then on to Quebec and the Gaspé Peninsula, where we spent the night of July 3 at St. Jean Port Joli. The next morning, Monday, July 4, we drove through New Brunswick to Edmundston and re-entered the United States at the small town of Madawaska, Maine. I am going into detail about the touring in Canada because it is important to my account that the reader knows I had been away from American contacts for several days. Leah and I seldom heard anything but French spoken while in Quebec Province. We decided to try to show how cosmopolitan we were, so we endeavored to use our own shaky French to communicate even with those who might have spoken English to us. We read no newspapers during that time. I had no radio in the small car I owned briefly at that time, and the only broadcasts we heard on occasional stops were in French.

From noon until evening on the Fourth of July we drove along U.S. 1 in a very rural part of Maine. We saw little traffic and few people, for all the stores in the small towns we passed through were closed for the holiday. The road was bumpy and in bad repair; however, we stopped and ate the tiny, delectable wild strawberries growing alongside the highway and felt very happy about the whole thing. Once we scared a bear cub into the bushes to his mama because we wanted to muscle in on his strawberry goodies. Another time we shared the highway with a large, many-horned stag for a few brief moments. Altogether it was a pleasant day in the wilds as we meandered along enjoying ourselves. Our mood was practically euphoric.

As we approached the Maine seacoast and the town of Machias, our destination for the night, I told my friend the story of Nelly Butler, the famous Machiasport ghost of 1799, whom I planned to investigate the next day. As it turned out, after our haunted night in Machias I was unable to write about Mrs. Butler for several months, and when I did finally prepare her story I did not mention anything about our personal adventure in her home territory. A writer who is emotionally too close to her material sometimes cannot discuss it at all.

Now, I must point out that while a ghost researcher should be objective and critical, she must also be willing to play the role of one who believes in ghosts if she hopes to attract them to her. A coldly rational disclaimer of their reality would certainly tend to negate the possibility of making any contact with anything of a supernormal nature, no matter what it is. Also, in improving my psychic ability I have sat in development classes frequently during the past fifteen years. I understand the proper procedures of opening my centers of awareness and receptivity, and am also aware of the necessity to protect myself against unwanted intrusions—whether psychological or spiritistic.

The more one knows, however, the less intelligently he practices it on occasion. So blithely oblivious to any possibility of danger from any other unseen source, I sent out a call several times during the day, addressed to the spirit of the late Mrs. Butler of Machiasport. I spoke aloud, broadcasting the word that we would be receptive to a visit from this spirit if, after all her years of inactivity, she should care to make herself evident to us in any way. Leah is also psychically developed, and she and I planned to hold a séance as soon as we were settled for the night. It never once occurred to us that any undesirable invisible entity on our wave-length might intercept our message and accept our invitation. Yet this may be what happened to us.

We arrived in Machias around 8:30 and found a large room in the new, modern Bluebird Motel on U.S. 1. Then we went out to dinner and returned at 10 o'clock. The moment I entered the motel room I began to feel light-headed, the initial stage of the trancelike condition that I sometimes achieve. I hurriedly prepared for bed, quite uncomfortably tired and dizzy. As I lay down on one of the two full-size beds in the room, I felt as if I might be taken into trance very easily and quickly.

Leah put all the lights out at my request, and then retired. But she jumped up immediately, walked across the room, and turned on the lamp in an alcove where the dressing table was. Although crabbiness is uncharacteristic of me, I insisted crossly that she turn off the light. Instead she draped a towel over it to darken the room and convinced me it was better that way.

Leah thought I was ready to go into trance and so did I. She suggested that we arrange a code—that if I "went out" I would return to myself immediately if she touched me and called my name. Leah said a prayer and asked that we be protected in whatever might occur, then we lay quietly in our beds and waited.

My head spun and I was approaching a condition of semi-consciousness as if I were being pulled forcibly into a whirlpool, when suddenly I became as cold as if exposed to an icy blast. My whole body was chilled inwardly as well as externally, and my stomach began to tremble with fright. With a strong effort I opened my eyes and sat up in bed, crying, "No, this is not right! I can't do it."

Leah also sat up, eager to agree with me. "I'm glad," she said. "I feel nervous, too. That's why I wanted the light on."

"Something evil is here," I said. Leah agreed vehemently.

"It's a bad influence of some kind," she said. "That is obvious. And I'm chilled to the bone."

I had not yet spoken about being cold, but I had experienced it *before* she mentioned it. We both felt some kind of negative presence in the room so strongly that we were badly frightened. We attempted to protect ourselves from its influence by repeating all the aphorisms for routing "evil spirits" that we could recall, and by praying and invoking the forces for good. Also, always a practical human being, I turned on the television and began to watch the "Johnny Carson Show," sure that laughter would bring me back to normal quicker than anything else.

Soon I was calmed down again, but it took my friend a while longer to regain her composure. She said that inwardly she kept hearing a voice saying, "It's all right. Why are you fighting it?" But she knew it was *not* all right and that she must fight. She walked up and down the room repeating protective statements. Finally she felt relieved of the oppression and went back to bed and to sleep very quickly.

I watched television until 12:30 and then, leaving lights on in the alcove and the bathroom, I finally managed to get to sleep.

Sometime later in the night I awoke in horror from a nightmare. I had dreamed that both Leah and I had been "taken over" by intruding malevolent spirits and we were yelling and acting most peculiarly. It seemed that we were so noisy that someone in the next room knocked on the door and told us to be quiet. As I awoke, an entity who had been bothering me and with whom I was myself somehow confused or identified, was talking to me or through me. I did not know whether it was a man or woman, but it was a powerful voice saying urgently, "I did *not* kill my children! It is all a mistake. I didn't do it!"

When I awoke I had the same frightened feeling of knots in my viscera and the cold chills I had experienced earlier that night. I had to fight the same way to control them and it took me quite a while. Eventually I slept again, not awakening until morning.

As Leah and I dressed and packed on the morning of July 5, I told her of my nightmare, and we discussed the events earlier in the night. Although we had no special reason to think there might be anything particularly significant about them, we decided they somehow were worth noting down. I wrote a complete report of the events and our emotions and reactions to them and signed my name to it. Underneath, Leah signed an attestation that the facts were true as they involved her and as I had reported my experiences to her.

After this notable notarizing act was accomplished, we left our room and went to the motel office to settle our bill. I told the manager's wife, Mrs. Barbara Manchester, that we were going to the nearby hamlet of Machiasport to try to learn more about the early American ghost who had appeared there so long ago. She had not heard anything about this famous apparition, but she kindly offered to telephone several members of the local Historical Society to ask them to help me. She was unsuccessful in finding anyone at home, so she began to give me directions for locating Machiasport.

Just then Leah came over to me with a newspaper in her hand. She had been glancing at that day's paper while I was talking to Mrs. Manchester. I said, "Not now, Leah, I'll read the news later." She insisted, "Look at this item. I think it has something to do with our experience."

The information contained in that newspaper and others that

I have since procured will be reported below. After looking at the paper, I gave the manager the handwritten account of our adventures of the night before to read. Then I wrote out another statement and asked Mrs. Manchester to sign it. It read: "I am witness to the fact that Miss Susy Smith has shown me a statement which she had written prior to coming into my office at 10 o'clock this morning. While in this office her friend discovered an article in the Tuesday, July 5, Bangor *Daily News* that she felt applied to her dream of last night." Signed, Barbara Manchester, July 5, 1966.

The newspaper article to which I refer told that Mrs. Constance Fisher, age thirty-seven, was being held without bail for the murder on Thursday, June 30, of her three children, Kathleen Louise, six, Michael Jon, four, and Nathalie Rose, nine months, by drowning. This same woman twelve years before had drowned her first three children, had been placed in a mental institution and later released to return to her husband. She had borne three more children and now had also killed them.

The story, in detail, as gleaned from other newspapers, is that on the afternoon of March 8, 1954, Carl Fisher, a railroad employee, had returned to his rural home on Rte. 23 between Fairfield and Hinckley, Maine, and found his wife unconscious and their three children dead. Beside Mrs. Fisher was a note that read: "God told me it was the only way to save them. . . ."

Mrs. Fisher was then placed in the Augusta State Mental Hospital, her condition described as an unnamed psychosis. After five years, in 1959, she was considered safe enough to be released. Her relatives were all warned to "come running" to the authorities at the least sign of a returning mental upset on her part; but none had done so. The Roman Catholic chaplain of Augusta State Hospital, the Reverend A. J. Lemire of the Oblate Fathers, said Mrs. Fisher had seemed all right when he last saw her, about fifteen months before.

Father Lemire stated, "I feel safe in saying there was no sign of any recurrence then. She was giving her children—two of them then—proper attention, bringing them up very nicely. The kids were happy, she was happy, and her husband was contented."

On Thursday afternoon, June 30, 1966, Carl Fisher came home from work to find his wife unconscious again and a note reading, "I'm sorry to have to do this. I haven't done a proper job in raising the children. They will be better off in Heaven." The bodies of two of his babies were tucked beneath a blanket on a bed; the third was found lying face down in a bathtub partially filled with water.

Both Leah and I could not help but feel that the agonized cries in my dream, "I did not kill my children," were somehow connected with Mrs. Fisher's case. How, we have been unable to analyze for certain, although we have considered almost every explanation and alternative. I have discussed the experience with several prominent parapsychologists, who find it highly interesting and say the story should be published; but they have no explanation for it. All suggestions, until we discussed it with those who have strong spiritualistic leanings, were negative as far as definite answers are concerned.

Among the interpretations that would be acceptable to psychical researchers was, of course, my possible subconscious knowledge of the situation involving Mrs. Fisher—or telepathy. Although I had read or consciously heard nothing about this case, which had been a *cause célèbre* in Maine over the Fourth of July weekend, could I have unconsciously glimpsed a headline? Perhaps I had overheard something in French about it and my meager knowledge of the language had translated the thoughts in my unconscious mind? (We must attribute to the subconscious mind inordinately clever powers it has never actually been proved to have, if we are to explain away psychic phenomena by normal means. But I am always willing to give it a try.)

Then again, if telepathy were the explanation, perhaps I had somehow tapped the "mental climate" in the state in such a way as to know about it telepathically in my dream. If the explanation is any of the above, though, why the chills and feeling of horror that accompanied the nightmare and that had also frightened both of us earlier in the evening?

Certainly the case represents more than merely two hysterical women trying to hold a séance and scaring themselves to death. We are both "old hands" at this sort of thing and have had numerous previous experiences with no such reactions. And our moods, as I have stressed, were blithe and cheerful as we went into the situation.

When I presented the facts of this case to my friend Charmienne (Chérie) Hughes, a psychic of intelligence and discernment, her interpretation of the events was interesting, if on the spiritualistic side. Certainly it brought the matter closer to ghosts, which is the topic with which we are at present involved. Chérie suggests that Mrs. Fisher was an unconscious medium who occasionally was possessed by a demented or at least highly confused and miserable earthbound spirit. Not understanding her condition and being very religious, when Mrs. Fisher heard a voice speaking to her she naturally thought it was God rather than a spirit entity. The fact that she was found unconscious each time the murders were committed indicates to a medium that Mrs. Fisher had gone into trance and was possessed while the deeds were done. Naturally she would then not be aware that she had personally been involved. And naturally then she would continue to utter her pathetic cry, "I didn't kill my children!"

If this could be the correct answer, then who was it that troubled Leah and me? Was it the entity who had left Mrs. Fisher now that she was in prison and was trying to extend his influence elsewhere? Chérie Hughes believes that when we made ourselves receptive and sent out calls to Nelly Butler, they were intercepted by this miserable soul, who answered and came to us. In that case, if it was this entity who had attempted to take me over earlier, how should my dream be interpreted? Was it he with whom I identified in the dream? Or might it have been Mrs. Fisher herself? The poor woman was probably in intense emotional turmoil in her jail cell. Great emotion can be conveyed telepathically to a receptive person. (No matter what those who do not know about this maintain, anyone who has studied ESP at all recognizes this as a fact.) Since my thoughts were tuned-in in this general direction, because of the advent of the malevolent entity earlier in the night, was I picking up Mrs. Fisher's inward reaction to the crimes when someone in my dream cried, "I didn't do it"?

Whatever the explanation, I still cringe inwardly as I recall that anguished cry, "It is all a mistake! I didn't kill my children!"

CHAPTER XIII

The C. Harvey W. Caper

DON'T LOOK NOW for the large, brownish-beige, Spanish-style house on N.W. 25th Avenue in Miami, Florida, surrounded by many tall and brooding trees. No longer does the huge oak nearly cover the front window, its leaves keeping the house in perpetual gloom. No more is the somber Florida room overhung by lofty avocado trees with their attendant dark green foliage. The house has been sold, remodeled, and painted a bright terra cotta; and all the beautiful and threatening trees have been cut down, leaving shockingly abrupt stumps in their place. A commonplace, inconspicuous house unadorned with verdure now, it is at present occupied by Cubans who speak no English. So there is no one to tell them of the harrowing history of their home, and of the ghost that haunted it so recently.

On the evening of February 25, 1962, Carrington Harvey Witherspoon, occupant of the above-mentioned residence in its pre-ravaged state, was preparing to break a chair over the head of his sixteen-year-old stepson, Kenny. Some apparent manifestation of careless love on the boy's part had aroused Mr. Witherspoon's ire. He was considerably put out. The expression of his displeasure was sufficient to distract his eight-year-old daughter, Betty, who up to that moment had been watching Soupy Sales on television. Pop was putting on a far better show. Mr. Witherspoon's performance also affected Mrs. Witherspoon, arousing in her the strongest maternal instincts. Excusing herself, she left the room and returned shortly with a .38 revolver. With this weapon she shot her husband through the heart, dead.

Carrington Harvey Witherspoon had been a violent man. Police records as quoted in the newspapers and the testimony of kindly neighbors bear this out. Mrs. Witherspoon had bought the revolver some time earlier to protect herself, and in Kenny's case it had certainly come in handy. Witherspoon in drink was particularly testy. On previous occasions he had smashed a $1,000 color television set with an ax (he ran the Harvey Electrical Company from the house and had probably got it wholesale); and he had dragged Mrs. Witherspoon around by the hair, shot at her with a shotgun, and several times threatened the lives of various members of the family. Mrs. Witherspoon had had him arrested from time to time. It had not been an ideal marriage.

Yet if the local gossip can be credited, it had been a going one. Some of the neighbors declared that Witherspoon had seemed like a fine person, that he was even a "good, clean-shaven man." Just what that is supposed to signify I cannot say, but that is the way the newspapers quoted them. It might mean that he was clean speaking or that he was close shaven. If the latter, Witherspoon definitely had one close shave too many.

Time passed. Mrs. Witherspoon was acquitted, doubtless on the forthright testimony of Witherspoon's cousin Vernon McCall, who, rip-roaring drunk, had arrived with Witherspoon on the fatal afternoon and had been gratuitously shot in the hand. So obstreperous was he in alcohol that he had to be forcibly removed in a "drunken tantrum" (quoting the newspaper once again) to Jackson Memorial Hospital where he was placed in restraint and held as a material witness.

Six months after the tragic contretemps, Mrs. Witherspoon

was subjected to more appalling grief when Kenny was killed riding his motorcycle. The accident occurred at the corner near the house, which, one would infer, now grew so distasteful to the poor mother that she disposed of it.

Some three years later, in 1965, Mrs. Gladys Chapman bought the house, including the wall-to-wall living-room carpeting with its two oval-shaped burn spots. These were, by and large, accepted as examples of Mrs. Witherspoon's marksmanship, together with the bullet hole in the front door. Conversation pieces, as it were, even though the killing was said to have occurred in the Florida room on the other side of the kitchen from the living room. Perhaps the shot marks presaged events to come. Anyway, in correspondence with her daughter, Mrs. C. Harvey White, who was in California, Mrs. Chapman wrote that "funny things are going on in this place."

A girl who lived with Mrs. Chapman said she also heard things she could not explain but decided it was just the understandable uneasiness of two women living in a gloomy old house over which hung the sinister shadow of a homicide. On March 26, Easter Sunday, 1967, Mrs. Chapman's daughter and her husband, Clayton Harvey White, arrived in Miami to live with Mrs. Chapman. The Whites took over the back bedroom, where they experienced no paranormal sensations whatever. But . . . shortly after her daughter arrived, Mrs. Chapman departed for California and the Whites moved into the front bedroom.

At this point it would seem pertinent to give an account of the White family, whose initials were identical to those of the Witherspoons. The men even had a middle name in common, by which both were known—Harvey. The Whites had two daughters, Janice, who was eleven, and Cheryl, eight at the time of this report. They also had three French poodles, Mimi, Gigi, and Suzette, who were normal dogs—lively, barking, running about and acting up over unfamiliar sounds made by strange dogs in the yard or strange humans at the door.

Mrs. White told me, after I was called in to help her, that she often has "a feeling" and knows when things are going to happen. She had not thought of the terms "psychic" and "sensitive" in connection with herself until I mentioned them. She had been more inclined to accept her husband's diagnosis that any unusual happenings she became conscious of were the figments of her imagination and nerves.

Nevertheless, when there were occasional loud, thudding crashes in the living room between two and three o'clock in the morning, Mr. White heard them along with his wife and the two children. The three poodles cowered, whimpering, under the bed. No running and barking for them when any phenomena were going on. Mr. White told me later that he knew these clamorous crashes were not the makings of his wife's imagination (but he made no attempt to explain to me what he thought they actually were). Bravely he had gone into the living room, but there was nothing unusual to be seen. He attempted to duplicate the noise in every way he could think of; but it was only when he fell heavily to the floor that the sounds were the same as those thuds that had awakened them all. To C. Harvey White's unobserving eyes on the nights of the crashes nothing was disturbed except the family and the dogs. But his wife maintains that the mirror and the pictures on the living-room walls were all found to be hanging crooked. (Would a woman be more likely to notice such things?)

Mrs. White has also heard the sound of chairs being moved in the Florida room (which was so gloomy it seldom performed its ostensible purpose of "sun" room in this house) and of someone walking around in the kitchen and moving things there. "I could sometimes feel something right beside me although there was nothing to see," she said. "And particularly in the Florida room I had cold chills and a feeling of evil. Occasionally at night I felt that someone was standing there, staring at me." A disturbance or two like that goes a long way; Mr. White's opinion of his wife's apprehensions would seem to have had some substance except for those crashes in the night, which he also heard.

Another thing: Mr. White spoke of a friend who had enjoyed

the hospitality of the back bedroom one weekend. He got up in the night for the usual reason and when he returned, his pillow had been fluffed up and placed at the foot of the bed. No one had any normal explanation for this extraneous room service.

Finally, in early May 1967, a woman whom the Whites had reluctantly permitted to use their address for her mail reported her car stolen. In the subsequent exchange with police who came to the door, Mrs. White mentioned to the officer in charge that she was also beset by invisible bogies. She thereby proved that "tell your troubles to a policeman" is an excellent precept. He promptly reassured her, "You must talk to Miss Susy Smith. She happens to live in the same apartment building that I do and knows all about such things as ghosts." Flattering, if a trifle overwhelming, but I accept it. Mrs. White did, too. She gave the officer her telephone number to be passed on to me; and the harassed woman was duly contacted via phone and her story duly noted.

Telephone conversations continued over a period of several days, as attempts proved ineffective to settle on a mutually agreeable date for us to get together. Then I let the matter drop for a while. A few weeks later, Mrs. White was sitting in the Florida room with a cup of coffee, reviewing in her mind the unexplained events that had taken place in the ill-fated dwelling since their tenancy. She reassured herself with, "You know there is *no* such thing as ghosts." No sooner had she thought this than, suddenly, she had a clammy feeling all over, chills up and down her spine, and there was a horrible, impossible-to-endure stench in the room.

Picking up the telephone, which was beside her chair, Mrs. White wasted not one moment calling her parapsychological mentor, and fortunately she found me in. I told her that such odors were often identified with haunted houses and that perhaps she should have a medium come and try to rid her of her ghost. She was very agreeable. "Enough is enough!" she said firmly.

On the night of May 31, 1967, I arrived at the N.W. 25th Avenue house with Harry Levy, a nonprofessional medium who was sure he could clarify the situation at the home of the C. Harvey W.'s. I had told him absolutely nothing about the Whites or their home, and I had warned them to say nothing to give the situation away. Good mediums, for the sake of genuine evidence, prefer to work without any previous briefing. Nonetheless, almost the first things that were pointed out to us in the house were the shot burns on the living-room carpet; and Harry soon knew all about the killing. He began, then, to get a mental picture that, he said, was of the murdered man. He reported that he was about thirty, vicious and cruel. The medium got "bad vibrations" in the Florida room, but agreed with Mrs. White that this was not the place where the shooting had occurred. Even though the newspaper stories had said it was, the neighbors insisted differently. Now Harry reinforced their arguments. He produced the name "James Thompson." He said, "There was a struggle for the gun. He was shot. He threatened her that even if he died he was going to come back and get even with her. He was a strong man." While possibly on the edge of the target, Mr. Levy's shots in the dark were nowise as accurate as those of Mrs. Witherspoon. Most of his statements were at variance with the newspaper reports, which fact, of course, does not necessarily incline the truth toward either Harry Levy or the newspapers.

Levy was then shown over the house and Mr. and Mrs. White recounted the experiences that had so disturbed them. Mrs. White related the events of one particular night when the two lights in the kitchen kept going on and off. They had done it before. In fact, she said, her mother had mentioned this in a letter as one of the peculiar symptoms of the house. But there was nothing wrong with the wiring; they had checked. This particular night after she had turned them off, the lights came on again several times in succession. She said she could see the toggles on the wall switches move as they were turned on, when no one was there to accomplish it manually. When I asked her how she could see this in the dark, she explained that the switches were near the door to the living room where they always kept a night light on. They also had a night light in the Florida room. No, she had no trouble telling what was going on. She just did not happen to approve of it. She said she finally got so angry that she announced aloud, "Look here, Witherspoon, I've had enough of this! Now cut it out!" Immediately the lights stopped acting up. Her husband called to ask her what was going on and who she was talking to.

"I've gone completely mad now," she answered. "I'm talking to the spook."

Harry Levy told Mrs. White further that he saw an old woman near her and the letter "V" was somehow associated with her. She then disclosed for the first time to either of us that she was called "Vangie" from her given name, Evangeline. The medium, however, preferred to associate the letter "V" with the old woman, and we did not argue with him.

At this time Harry sat down in the Florida room and began to hold mental communion with the spirit of C. Harvey Witherspoon. At least, he believed that was what he was doing. He reported to us later what had gone on. "You must leave this house," the entity was told; but a lot of arguing ensued. "No, you have to go away," Harry said he was firm. "You no longer live here and you shouldn't bother the people who now own your old home." Harry said it was most difficult to get through to the spirit because he was so miserable and was such an unenlightened soul. The medium was quite discouraged, for he did not feel that he had been able to improve the situation at all. As we left, he urged Vangie White to call him at any time, day or night, if she had any further trouble of any kind with her ghost. I, too, had no thought that we had been of help. Harry and I were not in a hopeful frame of mind as we drove off.

That same night, however, about 12:45 Mrs. White woke up suddenly. She had the usual cold, funny feeling that she had previously experienced when the ghost was there. She did not see him, but she was strongly aware of his presence. Then she began for the first time to hear him speak. It was not an actual sound heard aurally, but a very strong mental impression in which she was aware of the words in her mind as mediums are— I have already noted that Mrs. White was highly psychic. Then she began to realize that the spirit she thought to be Witherspoon was crying. It sounded as if he were near enough to touch her as he said, "Please let me stay here. I have no place to go."

"No. We don't want you," she told him. "Go away!"

He blubbered, "But I built this house. I don't want to leave." She insisted that he go, and this repartee continued for quite a while. Mrs. White became colder and more unnerved, and finally she bolted for the telephone and called Harry Levy. "What'll I do?" she cried, as he answered. "He's right here crying and talking to me."

"The only thing you can do is to convince him he must leave," the medium told her. "If he is talking to you and crying that is a very good sign. I think everything will be all right now."

Harry had hit it that time, right on the noggin. When Vangie returned to bed, her ghost was gone. And, to my knowledge, he has remained gone ever since. Certainly the Whites had no more evidence of his presence while they lived in the house. No more bumps in the night; no more cold chills; no more cowering, whimpering dogs; and no more lights flashing on and off.

Poor, violent Carrington Harvey Witherspoon, if indeed it was he, bumbling about the house, not realizing that his home no longer belonged to him. What would he say if he saw it now, in its denuded state? Somehow I cannot help but compare Witherspoon with those trees cut down in their prime, remaining only as ugly stumps. Let us hope that Vangie White's efforts set him free of the house and released him, regenerated, to soar with grace toward some kind of a heavenly home.

CHAPTER XIV

The Curse
of the Bell Witch

IN 1817 AN ENTITY which came to be known as the Bell Witch moved in on the prosperous Tennessee farmer John Bell and his family and for four years tortured and persecuted them with unrelenting fury. In *Prominent American Ghosts* I gave the most complete account yet published of the Bell Witch and its activities, researching every historical document about the old case. Since the publication of that book I have had the opportunity to meet a descendant of the original John Bell and to learn further data which promote his belief that the Bell Witch has struck again!

In the chapter in my earlier book entitled "The Bell Witch," the many persecutions are enumerated and described as this invisible ghost or poltergeist that called itself a witch teased and harassed members of the family and their friends and neighbors. It centered much of its attention on John Bell's daughter, Betsy, and made her life miserable with hair pullings, pinchings, and slappings. It also stuck pins into her and mistreated her generally. Kate, as the witch called herself, played pranks on almost everyone else indiscriminately, but she hated John Bell. For him there was no tomfoolery, but only destructive acts of violence.

Eventually John Bell came down with an illness during which he complained of a curious sensation in his mouth, a stiffness of the tongue, and something like a stick crosswise, punching each side of his jaws. As time went on this affliction increased, his tongue swelling against his jaws so that he could neither talk nor eat for ten or fifteen hours at a time. John Bell died in agony, and Kate took full credit.

After this Betsy Bell gave up fighting the witch and canceled her engagement to Josh Gardner, for that was what Kate most seemed to want her to do. This, along with John Bell's death, broke the witch's hold on the family. She had no more reason to stay around, and gradually she made her presence felt less and less. She spoke one night and said she would be gone for seven years, and she was.

Betsy Bell married the schoolteacher Dick Powell, but he only lived for seventeen years longer. Betsy remained a widow for the rest of her life, and died at the age of eighty-six. Although she was high spirited, entertaining, industrious, and goodna-tured (as well as quite stout), she was always plagued by the misrepresentation of her role in the Bell Witch's activities. Some persons maintained to the end that Betsy herself had been the instigator of all the naughtiness attributed to Kate, and had been the cause of her father's death.

When the witch returned after seven years it was to the family of John Bell, Jr., that she made herself evident. She did nothing unpleasant then, but she promised to return in one hundred and seven years to haunt the family. At that time, she said, she would be the bearer of evil tidings for Tennessee and the whole nation.

John Bell, Jr., and his siblings and their descendants lived out their lives, and one hundred and seven years passed away. Came 1935, the year when "Kantankerous Kate" had promised to re-turn. The report written by Dr. Charles Bailey Bell, entitled

The Bell Witch, a Mysterious Spirit, stated that the witch did not show up to keep her rendezvous with modern members of the Bell family. So *Prominent American Ghosts* concluded its account with: "But 1935 came and went with no sign of her. Descendants of John Bell heaved justifiable sighs of relief."

Now comes new information. In Gulfport, Mississippi, in the spring of 1969, I was introduced to a Bell offspring named Robert Borden Adam, known to his friends as Robin. He was quick to disenchant me about the Bell Witch, telling me of the tragic deaths in his immediate family and of his belief that they definitely indicate that the Witch's Curse is still in effect. Robin's mother, Ann Bell Adam, whom we mentioned as having seen an apparition in the chapter entitled "The Doctor's Dilemma," was a daughter of John Elijah Bell II of Tennessee. She was a member of the generation living in that crucial year designated by the witch—1935.

John Elijah Bell I, Robin's Grandfather Bell's father, was a prominent lawyer in Memphis. His death was sudden enough and violent enough to comply with a witch's curse, whether or not it might have been merely an accident. He was killed while walking across a street, being hit by an ambulance rushing someone else to the hospital.

In the winter of 1969 Robin's Grandmother Bell, widow of John Elijah II, had a strange death very similar to the suffering of the original John Bell. I talked to her doctor in Gulfport, who told me Mrs. Bell died very peculiarly of a mysterious nerve ailment. It was diagnosed as possible amotrophic lateral sclerosis. Particularly curious, in the light of the first Bell's symptoms, was Mrs. Bell's complaint of stiffness in her throat and mouth and the fact that she could not talk. When her death came it was very rapid and totally unexpected at the time.

Robin's father was Attorney Robert B. Adam, known as Bobby. He was a short, stocky, jolly man. His wife, Ann Bell Adam, was a tall, slender, effervescent brunette. Their oldest daughter, Sally, was married. Two other daughters, who lived at home, were Mary Cannon (Nan), age eighteen, and Margaret (Peggy), age eight. On the night of January 25, 1968, Robin, who was twenty-one, was in Navy boot camp in San Diego, California. His account of the night the Bell Witch first struck his family follows:

"I was awakened and told to hurry and get dressed because I had a telephone call. Then as I was walking toward the phone I was told that my father had been killed. It shook me something terrible, but I managed to get to the phone. When I talked to my mother she told me the rest of the horrible story. My dad and my two younger sisters had been burned to death in a fire in our home. The Navy started processing me immediately and got me on a plane in two and a half hours. When I arrived home in Gulfport, Mother told me the details of what had happened.

"She had waked up about maybe 3:30 and heard this crackling sound in the house. She started to go down the hall to see what it was, but when she opened the door fire poured into the room. She closed the door, shrieking for my father. He awoke and groggily ran out through the sliding glass doors along the side of the room to try to alert the girls. Mother was dialing the fire department but before she could reach them the flames almost engulfed her. She darted through the glass doors and got caught in the curtains and fell, sure she was a goner; but fortunately she landed outside the curtains and was saved.

"Mother ran around the house to the windows of my youngest sister's room and tried to get in. Daddy was there and told her to go on, he would get Peggy. Mother then ran around to the front to Nan's room. She started beating on the windows trying to break in. She did manage to shatter the glass, and cut her hands badly, but they were those eight-pane casement windows that crank open and she couldn't possibly have gotten through them. The awful irony of it was that Mother went to the wrong windows. There was one that I knew about that would have opened easily.

"Mother could see Nan lying on the floor by the phone. She

turned around and raced toward a man out on the street, screaming for him to help her get her baby out of the room. The man
instead threw Mother on the ground and held her to keep her
from running into the flaming house. Just about then the fire
reached Dad's ammunition that he kept to load his gun collection. As it exploded the fire shot three hundred feet into the air,
according to a policeman who arrived just before the fire department got there.

"Daddy had gone around and entered my bedroom, which
was occupied at the time by a maid Mother had brought up from
Mexico. He got her out and went on through the house to
Peggy's room. He picked up my little sister in his arms and
rushed to the window; but when he broke it open the fire and
smoke were drawn through that vent and they were killed in-
stantly. Yolanda, the maid, and Mother were the only ones who
escaped the fire."

As to how this holocaust started there are many conjectures,
but nothing is known for certain. Although it seems to have
begun in the area near the water heater, it could not have been
that which caused it because the heater was later found to be
intact. It has been suggested that some electrical equipment had
malfunctioned and begun to smolder and then finally burst into
flame. This does not seem logical to Robin because of the time
element. Bobby and Ann had company that night for dinner.
The guests left at 1:30. Sometime between 1:30 and the time
Ann first discovered the fire, Nan came home from a date. She
could not have been in long, however, for her bed had not yet
been slept in. If Nan had walked into a house in which there
had been fire smoldering she surely would have smelled it, for
the apparent seat of the fire was right near her room.

Because Robert B. Adam, Sr., had been a lawyer, who might
have had enemies among those whom he had necessarily antag-
onized during trials, there were local rumors to the effect that
perhaps he had been murdered—that the fire had been set by
someone with a grudge. The fire was set, all right, according to

his son, Robin. It was set by that same invisible entity who had plagued his family so bitterly in the past—the Bell Witch.

Robin stayed with his mother almost a month. Then he returned to camp. He saw her three or four times after that. She was emotionally upset, of course, but he did not at any time hear her threaten to kill herself. She was apparently considering it constantly, however.

On May 5 Ann called a friend and said, "I've taken sleeping tablets."

"Good," said the friend. "You need a long night's sleep."

"I've taken eighty-seven of them," said Ann. Even with all the help that was immediately rushed to her, Ann Bell Adam died two nights later.

Her son is positive the Curse of the Bell Witch was in operation in her life, possibly even in her suicide.

"I couldn't say whether it has caused all that has happened so far," he told me, "but I do believe it has returned. I'll probably believe in it until the day I die." He wonders about the other branches of the Bell family, but he does not have any direct contact with them, so he does not know if they have had any serious troubles recently that seem unusual enough to be attributed to Kate's activities.

Robin does not like to expect a large amount of grief for himself, but he is not discounting the possibility that it may come to him and his. For this reason, when he was courting his wife he insisted she read a copy of Dr. Charles Bailey Bell's paper before she gave him her answer to his proposal of marriage. He did not want her to marry him under any false hope of his being able to give her a carefree and curse-free life. She read it, and she told me that she did worry about it a bit. But Robin's charm won out, and finally she accepted him in spite of the Curse of the Bell Witch.

Her name, incidentally, is Betsy.

CHAPTER XV

The Case of
the Pregnant Angels

CAN THE GHOSTS of an old couple who loved an estate become fond of the new owners and remain to participate in their activities? There seems to be evidence that such is the case in the bobbing chandeliers, flickering lights, apported angels, and other unexplainable phenomena at Denver's Bradmar. Perhaps it is the fact that Dr. Robert Bradley and his wife and sons love their Tudor manor so much and are intent upon improving it to the point of perfection that has inspired this continuing interest from the other side. Whatever the reason, the haunts have apparently remained during all the seven years since the Bradleys moved in, and they do not seem about to leave. This house is one place where we are forced to face the curious fact that if ghosts do not exist, then something else just as inexplicable does.

In addition to the invisible entities, the cast of characters involved here consists of Dr. Robert A. Bradley, a Colorado obstetrician and gynecologist who has achieved worldwide fame through his books, papers, and lectures advocating natural childbirth. Bob is an extra-large, nice-looking man with a disarming Western breeziness and an advocacy of his own enthusiasms that can sometimes be a bit overwhelming. His wife, Dorothy Bomar Bradley, is a charming, handsome woman with a dramatic way of speaking that reveals her interest in local theatrical productions—in which she has taken some highly successful leading roles. She is also a very talented sculptress. The couple has three splendid, nonhippie sons: Philip, age twenty-one, Pelham, nineteen, and Parris, sixteen. Their pets are a middle-aged poodle named Tout Suite and a Doberman pinscher pup named Desdemona.

Also living with the Bradleys in their roomy home is Dr. Siegwalt Palleske, professor of foreign languages at the University of Denver. Dorothy's cousin, Karl Vogel, an interior designer, also lived in the house until recently; and when I visited them her attractive sister, Bernadette Thorn, of Los Angeles was there. It is the high caliber of all these interesting, cultured people that adds so much to one's tendency to accept the accounts they give about the peculiarities of their house.

The story of how Bradmar came to belong to the Bradleys opens the sequence of events to be reported here. It is the only part that is not spooky. Dorothy and Bob and the boys, along with Sieg, who is a permanent family fixture, were living in a comfortable Denver house in which Bob thought they would spend the rest of their days, when Dorothy happened to accept an invitation to take a ride with a friend who was a real estate agent. Bob was lecturing in Canada and when he returned the whole family met him at the airport, a most unusual occurrence.

"We want to buy a house," they cried almost in unison as soon as he was settled in the car.

"We have a house. Are you out of your minds?" he asked.

They took him for a ride, nonetheless, and showed him the prize they had discovered. Right in the midst of the outskirts of the city of Denver is a large and exclusive area owned by only a few individuals and containing a mere handful of houses. The car turned into a road on this property and drove through vacant fields waist high in grass, up a road over which giant cottonwood trees leaned protectively. Bob wondered what had come over his family when he saw the hulking, deserted white-elephant of a house with twenty rooms plus half a dozen baths. With its hundred or so broken windowpanes, it had obviously been overrun by vandals numerous times during the year it had been vacant since its former owner's death. Bob was appalled at its condition. But as soon as he stepped inside the great hall with its windows clear to the gabled roof, even as he scuffed through the dirt and trash on the floor, the house claimed him as it had his wife and sons.

"There was a quiet feeling of security here," Bob told me, "and a certainty that it would be ours."

The new house was named "Bradmar" for Bob's Bradley and Dorothy's Bomar, and a massive job of restoration began. It has taken a long time because it was in such deplorable condition, and also because the Bradleys are such perfectionists; so improvements are still going on today. No time or expense is spared to make each addition or substitution exact and correct, and to find the proper antiques with which to furnish it.

The house had originally been designed by one of the best architects of its day and built in 1920 as a wedding present for the daughter of a wealthy Denver family. The bricks were hand-made English imports, as were the enormous hinges on the three-inch-thick solid-oak doors. This lady lived in and loved the house; but when her husband died she sold it. Later she married again and her second husband bought it back and surprised her with it as an engagement gift. They lived there together ever after. Do they still?

As he was having the gold swan-shaped bathroom fixtures installed, Bob told his sons, "I am putting every cent I own into this house to make it as faultless as possible. If you boys let it go or allow it to deteriorate after I die you'll see such haunting as you never would have believed!"

When they bought the house it had no reputation for ghosts but only an unusual story that the Bradleys began to hear from various persons who visited them. There is one beam in the ceiling of the drawing room that has a most peculiar series of splits for its full length. They are deep gashes, but they occur in a number of small, incomplete, angled cracks in the center portion of the wood and do not follow through with the pattern of the grain to the edges as one would logically expect. Thus the breaks do not weaken the beam as a support. The drawing room is immense, and the beams which cross its width from the huge fireplace to the wall are thirty feet long, fifteen inches deep, and eighteen inches high. The wood in the center of the gashes is not dried out, so the splits could not have been in the beam when the house was originally constructed forty-five years before. In fact, the cracks hardly looked more than a year old when the Bradleys moved into the house.

The former caretaker of the property was the first to repeat the story of the beam, and later as friends came in to see the house it was frequently related again. It seems that after the passing of her second husband, the former owner lived for seventeen years alone with her servants. Before she died she told them, as well as various friends and relatives, that she wanted her casket to be placed in front of the fireplace in the drawing room for her funeral services. There is nothing unusual in this. In those days it was quite popular to be brought home to lie in state in your own parlor. But then, as a sign, she said she would cause the large beam above it to split from end to end. This is just what occurred with a loud detonation while her coffin lay there in the house. A servant of the former owner has since told the Bradleys that she was adjusting the hair of her late mistress at the moment that the beam resounded like a rifle shot and the splits appeared.

Karl Vogel, in his capacity as member of the family as well as interior decorator, has been supervising the restoration. He loves and admires the house as much as the others do. He told me that, needing to be sure that the split beam would be strong enough to support the ceiling after the addition of a number of big men to the household, he brought in a group of experts for their opinions.

"I had here all at the same time," he said, "a building engineer, an architect, a general contractor, and a roofer—a gutter specialist in case the possibility of rain seeping in could have caused the cracks. They checked everything carefully and then all agreed that the beam would be strong enough to hold any increase in weight. They also agreed that the split was fresh, because it had not dried out inside; but not one of them had an idea of how the beam had become damaged in the first place.

"After being satisfied that these people, who were all professionals, could not explain it, I told them the story I'd heard from the caretaker and later from some friends about the former owner and how she apparently caused the beam to split after her death. They all admitted that this explanation was as good as any they had to offer."

It was not long before the people working in the house began to realize that incidents were continually occurring that could not be accounted for normally. Karl Vogel took with great skepticism all the statements he heard about peculiar events. He'd had no experience whatever with haunts up to the time the work started, and had little patience with such theories. Even when he began to face the fact that all kinds of odd and unnatural things were happening to the electrical system, he still did not accept them as any kind of supernormal manifestations. It was not until he had his personal adventure one moonlight night that his thinking about the whole subject changed.

There was so much work to be done on the house that it was still unfinished when school opened in the fall. In order for the boys, who were aged from nine to fourteen then, to be enrolled in the new school it was necessary for the Bradleys to prove that they occupied the house. The fact that members of the family were working there all day long was not adequate evidence. The children had to be sleeping there. For this reason it was necessary for the different male members of the family to take turns staying with them, sharing what the boys considered to be the excitement of sleeping in the big, empty house.

So that subsequent events can be understood, it should be explained here just how Bradmar is laid out. The great hall with its accompanying entrance halls separates the house into two complete wings, connected on the second floor by a balcony that crosses the stairwell. In the wing over the drawing room and the solarium, where the pool table is, are Dr. Bob's and Dorothy's suites. The wing on the other side of the house contains on the first floor the library, dining room, butler's pantry, and kitchen, and Sieg's and the guests' suites upstairs. Extending on past the kitchen are a breakfast room, utility rooms, halls, and the back entrance. The servants' quarters, which are now the boys' bedrooms, are above them.

When the distance from Dorothy's room at the far southern end of the second floor to the back door at the far northern end of the house downstairs is considered, it hardly seems possible that the back door slamming could be heard there. Yet in a completely empty house this was definitely the case, I am assured by everyone involved.

Here is Karl Vogel's account of his escapade the first night he slept there:

"Because the floors were being sanded it was necessary that we all camp in the big room that is now Dorothy's bedroom. The boys had boxspring mattresses on the floor, and I was to sleep on a cot. Long after they had gone to sleep I was sitting on the edge of my bed for a last cigarette, thinking about the work that was to be done the next day, and looking out the windows admiring the moonlight and the shadows that were falling through the trees. As I tamped out my cigarette I heard the back door closing. Although it is in the other wing, far from the room where I was, the slam resounded through that empty house. Now, I had very carefully locked all the doors before I came upstairs. I knew no one could get in without a key. Because it was my first night to bunk there, Dr. Bradley or Palleske could have dropped by to see how we were getting along, so I was not disturbed at first. But then I began to hear footsteps, and they were not like the men's footsteps at all. It was a soft-toed sound almost like the soft-soled fabric bedroom slippers our grand-mothers used to wear. They were not distinct steps but a scoot ... a shuffle. With all that dirt on the floor the scratchy scuffling was even more distinct.

"I got up and walked down the hall, calling out 'Bob' and 'Sieg!' There was no answer. Then I approached the balcony and looked down into the great hall below. Its marble floor was beautiful, flooded as it was with moonlight, yet eerie in that empty and dirty house. All the while those scuffling footsteps had been coming closer. Finally they entered the hall—but there was no one there and nothing to be seen. Well, I have to admit that I was ... it was ... well, it scared the hell out of me, is what it did! The steps would scuttle and then stop for a little bit and then scuttle onward. They never did cross into the drawing room, but seemed to stay right there in the hall below me. I got this weird tingling sensation or chill, standing there looking down at *nothing*, and yet hearing it walk across the floor. Well, finally I said to myself, 'This is ridiculous!' And in my fright I bellowed out, 'All right, Ethel, if that's you, if you don't like the way I'm doing this damned house you'd better let me know or it'll be too late.' ——"

I stopped Karl Vogel abruptly right in the middle of his ac-count. "Ethel?" I asked. "Is that the name of the woman who owned the house before?" Everyone there had been careful not to mention her name to me and I had been pledged not to try to learn the family name and use it, because no unpleasantness with her offspring was desired. Yet when I heard the name "Ethel" I had a momentary shock because of something I had personally experienced in the house.

On my first day there I had thought I heard someone calling "Ethel." I noticed this particularly for a very special reason. I was born Ethel Elizabeth Smith and it was not until I was in college that people began calling me "Susy." I have since adopted Susy as my legal name, and will not allow my childhood friends to call me Ethel even when they might still have a tendency to do so. I had known the Bradleys for only a short time and was quite sure they had no information about my early life. Anyway, the call was a vague, more cerebral than external, sensation, so I had put it aside, thinking, "No one here knows my name was Ethel so they can't be calling me." I mentioned this to no one and it was completely out of my thoughts until Karl revealed the name in his story. Now I wondered, as did the rest of the Bradleys when I told them, just which Ethel it was that I had heard being called the day before. It adds a bit to the mystery of the house, as far as I am concerned.

Karl Vogel went on, saying that no one had answered his challenge and not a sound was heard in the big, luminous hall. He stood there a while, but the ghost outwaited him, and so he finally went back to his bed. He lay there wondering if he was cracking up, and then gradually he began once more to plan his work for the next day. Then he heard the footsteps again, and now they were retreating from the hall, going farther and farther away. Then the back door slammed.

"I really did get quite shook up inside about it," Karl said. "I lay there rolling and turning all night, thinking, 'This has got to be the screwiest thing I've ever run into.' I could hardly wait until the next morning to check with the family; but when I did I was assured the men had not been there."

The Bradleys were later to write about Karl's experience: "The morning after Karl's first turn, his disbelief in things paranormal came to an abrupt end. We all chuckled at the expression on his face, it so resembled ours at the time we were introduced to personal experiences of this nature. . . ."

Yes, Dorothy and Bob had had unusual psychic occurrences before during their thirty years of married life, and since buying Bradmar they had become real enthusiasts about psychical research. In 1967 they wrote a book together about their interest, called *Psychic Phenomena: Revelations and Experiences.* In it they said: "One often reads of similar, unexplained ... happenings occurring to others and dismisses them with a shrug of skepticism. Surely, one says, these happenings can be traced to hallucinations, practical jokes, trickery, fraud, etc. But let it happen to you, just *once* let it happen to you! It takes only one white crow to prove that all crows aren't black. It may take only one clear-cut thing without a known explanation, happening to you personally, when you are convinced that no fraud or trickery could have been involved, to start you on a train of thought in search of an explanation."

Karl Vogel had begun to take a ride on the Bradleys' train of thought. Some of the electrical incidents he had made light of earlier now took on new meaning for him. He recalled the first day that Clifford Mueller, the electrician, had worked for them there. Karl had discovered that like most houses built in the 1920's, Bradmar was underpowered and the electrical wiring did not have the circuitry that he felt was necessary. So most of the old wiring was pulled out and new and heavier wiring installed, and a great deal more power was brought into the house to carry the load.

On the first day that Mueller arrived to do this work, Dorothy, Karl, and Philip were peeling the green wallpaper off the guest bedroom walls when the light in the ceiling suddenly went on. A yellow bug bulb was in the socket, and the wallpaper immediately took on a seasickly, jaundiced hue. Dorothy, standing in the center of the room, exclaimed, "Who turned on this hideous yellow light?" It was obvious that no one had, however, because Philip was on a stepladder across the room from the wall switch and Karl was standing right beside Dorothy. No one had passed the door, either, yet the light button on the wall was turned to "On." Dorothy called out to the electrician to ask what he had done that might cause the light to come on. His muffled voice responded, "Nothing. I'm in the linen closet getting supplies."

That was the first of it. Soon the bell system in the house went crazy. Bells still peal in the middle of the night on occasion. The front doorbell—an eight-note Westminster chime—goes off when no one is there to ring it. The annunciator in the kitchen buzzes to tell some invisible maid of a former day to bring breakfast to her unseen mistress. In the seven years the Bradleys have lived at Bradmar the various bells have rung wildly at any and all times, yet there is nothing wrong with their wiring.

"The entire wiring system in the house is now adequate and in good condition," Karl told me. "It was done by a very reputable man and has been checked and rechecked."

This reputable man, an electrician for twelve years who has encountered no such troubles elsewhere, did not believe in psychical phenomena when he went to work at Bradmar. He is not even sure how much he believes about it now.

"All I know," Clifford Mueller declared to me with emphasis, "is that these things happened. I have worked around that house before they moved in, I worked there up in the attic with the bats for a period of time and when I was alone I saw no indications of unusual activity. I am not averse to working in that house alone. I have no fears. I don't know what caused the phenomena. But I do know that they occurred."

Siegwalt Palleske, who was not too much of a believer himself, but who has now encountered much that he cannot explain normally, suggested to me that perhaps it is the combination of several psychic people in the house that makes these phenomena possible. He does not have these experiences with others, but he definitely has them there with Dorothy and Bob. "It may be that all three of us are somewhat sensitive," he said to me.

Dorothy told about one occasion when they had just finished completely rewiring the last wing of the house and the electrician had assured her on leaving that afternoon, "It's all fixed!" However, in the evening when they brought friends to show them through the house not a light in that particular wing would go on. The next day she indignantly called the electrician back on the job, and he spent the remainder of the morning try-ing to determine the source of the trouble.

Dorothy said, "Around noon, as the men were breaking for lunch, I was coming through the hall and I saw him walking down the stairs, muttering to himself. He seemed completely unaware of my presence and continued to speak only to him-self. I was able to catch the words, 'It isn't possible, but I saw it!' 'I *know* it isn't possible.' 'I've never seen such a thing in my life!' "

"What's the problem?" asked Mrs. Bradley. Mueller told her that he had searched all morning to find the cause of the trouble, from the basement to the attic, and finally, in desperation, he had pulled the newly connected wires out of the metal conduits. That was when he found to his utter amazement that the braided cable that he had carefully fed through the conduit and prop-erly connected and had working the day before was now un-braided, scrambled, and disconnected.

Two days later the electrician was faced with another prob-lem. Sieg and Dorothy were in the boys' wing of the house, Doro-thy in the back room and Sieg in the hallway, up on a ladder sanding some woodwork with a rented electric hand-sander. Dorothy says: "I was startled to hear a groan and a crash. I rushed out to find Sieg sitting on the floor holding his head. He looked up bewildered and asked indignantly, 'Did you hit me?' I answered, 'Of course I didn't hit you. Besides, I was in the back room!' Sieg removed his hand from his head long enough to ask me, 'Am I bleeding?' "

Dorothy reassured him that he was not bleeding; but there was a large round red area on his right temple. She kept asking Sieg what had happened, and when he became more collected he told her that at the moment he had been hit on the head the sander had stopped working. He wondered if perhaps a short circuit in the machine had caused the blow. Since the short would have had to detour his arm and jump through the air to hit him in the temple only, this did not seem likely. And besides, electrical shocks would not be apt to make a localized bruise like that. At least they did not think it would. They quickly made their way downstairs to find their harassed electrician to learn if such a thing were possible.

According to Dorothy, "He backed away warily and said, 'No.' Then I asked him if he would please make the sander work again. He tried it, and it did not work for him either. He removed the casing, took it apart, found no problem, turned it on, and it worked. He replaced the casing, turned it on—and it did not work! He took it off again, looked at it, turned it on—it worked. He replaced the casing—turned it on—it would not work. This pattern continued for a while. Later, I was delighted to see a professional union electrician sitting, spraddle-legged, beating the sander repeatedly against the floor. He was the picture of frustration. 'I thought that was the way we amateurs fixed things,' I said, 'not you professionals.'"

"Yes," Mueller told me when I checked all this with him, "these things happened. I don't know what caused them. They do not happen anywhere else I have ever worked, but they happen here." When he works at Bradmar, he has learned to keep his cool. This is a favorite place of his, but his motto here now is, "Don't fight it!"

Bob Bradley was talking to me about how the lights have always gone on and off from time to time in the house, whether or not the switches were moved. "This intrigued me," he said, "why the switch would work by itself at one time and at other times the lights would go on without the switch moving. We had both of these happen while the electrician was here. Also, later on at night members of our family had heard footsteps walking through the house and this was concomitant with lights going on and off."

Dr. Bob then told me a great story about how he learned what was causing this—and then corroborated it. He said that in 1962 shortly after they had moved into Bradmar he was at a hypnosis convention in Philadelphia and had the opportunity to meet the famous medium Arthur Ford, who lives in that city. They had never met before; *Psychic Phenomena* had not yet been written; and Ford had no idea who Bob was when he asked for a private sitting. Yet the medium no sooner went into his trance than Fletcher, his control, said, "I see you live in a large home out west. It is enormous with many rooms."

Then the doctor was startled to hear Fletcher add, "The lights go on and off and there are the sounds of footsteps walking through this house." Bob wondered how he could have known that unless by telepathy. But then Fletcher immediately went beyond anything he could have acquired from Bob's mind by giving an explanation for this. He said that an elderly couple had lived by themselves there for a long time and that *she* liked the place completely dark. She had kept all the blinds pulled even though this house has many windows and is a bright, cheerful home, so that it was constantly dark day and night. Her husband did not care for this and when he would stumble on a chair or something he couldn't see he would flounce through the house in anger snapping on lights. Then she would come along right behind him and snap them off. Fletcher added, "They are still doing this."

"It sounds like a good explanation," I remarked to Dr. Bradley. "But how could you know whether or not it was true of these people?"

"As soon as I got home we checked it out. We learned the whereabouts of one of the former owner's servants, who had been the head housekeeper, and we invited her to come over to see how we had redone the house. Almost the first thing she said when she walked in was, 'My, how nice and bright it is. My mistress kept the shades pulled down and it was always so dark in here!' "

Bob asked her if the lady and her husband had quarreled about the darkness and she verified that they did. "They were constantly flipping the lights on and off," she said.

Probably Dr. Bradley's most exciting single experience in the house occurred early one morning. In order to get to the hospital in time to perform his surgery, he usually leaves home by six-thirty or seven. This morning he descended the stairs, reached in his pocket for a cigar, and walked into the drawing room to use the heavily weighted lighter that rested on a marble-topped table. He says, "As my hand approached it, I was startled to see the lighter gently rise and float about a foot away, coming silently to rest on its side. In bewilderment I examined it minutely; there were no strings attached or anything else that could have caused it to move. Everyone else in the house was still asleep upstairs, so there was no one around who might be playing pranks on me, if such a thing had been possible under those conditions. I spent the next half hour tipping that lighter over in every way I could think of. No matter how slowly it was pushed off balance, it would always fall noisily with a metallic clink, not silently."

As I have already mentioned, enough of such experiences are convincing. Dr. Bob has had enough of them and he is definitely convinced. But what of the cultured, enlightened modern scholar, Siegwalt Palleske, who has become involved in these events just because he associates himself so closely with the Bradleys in their home environment? Sieg told me he is much more of a skeptic than they are, probably because he is not nearly as psychically sensitive, and not as much has happened to him personally. And yet, even for him, "A lot of things have occurred that I've just had to accept." He cannot explain them, but he knows they have happened. There was one especially odd occurrence with lamps that turned themselves on and off at the other house where Sieg and the Bradleys lived before they moved into Bradmar. There has never been a logical explanation, either, for the jolt on Sieg's temple that knocked him off the stepladder.

Sieg is inclined to try to figure some normal way the lights can flicker on and off at Bradmar, however, rather than accepting the possibility that the ghosts are doing it. The lights in the library, for instance, that fluctuate so often, can they not be caused by some apparatus in the house, he wonders—the automatic stoker of the furnace, for instance? And yet even as he raised this question Sieg recalled that the same phenomena occur in the summer when the furnace is not in use.

He also mentioned the incident that Bernadette, Dorothy's sister, had told me about. The two sisters had been meditating one night in the library and had spoken of their grandmother. Bernadette said, "I can't remember exactly what I said, but it was something about our grandmother having been so close to us—she raised me—and we were wondering if she was ever around us now. At that moment those lights in the chandelier flared up bright. After they went down again Dorothy made some funny remark, I've forgotten just what, about Grandmother and her sense of humor . . . what she would have said about that situation . . . something like that. The lights flared up again. They are usually kept fairly dim with a rheostat, but this night they flared brightly at those specific moments."

Sieg said in discussing this, "Oh, it is an interesting thing, all right, particularly because they do seem to flicker at significant times. At other times they haven't flickered at all for hours and hours. But I'd like to have more tests made involving them, that's all."

Later that night I was in the library when the lights flared briefly on several occasions, as if in agreement with certain comments in the conversation. I checked with Sieg when I came out, to see if other lights in the house had also done this. If it were any of the apparatus going on or off, or even any fluctuation in the current coming into the house, it should have flickered in all the lights, not just the ones in the library. Sieg said the rest had behaved perfectly naturally.

Another occasion on which the lights in the chandelier in the library had acted particularly insanely was when an Englishwoman had been a guest in the house. She was very sensitive and was said to have worked for years with psychic development groups. The moment she walked into the library, Bob told me, the lights practically danced. During the entire time she was there they flickered, flaring up bright and then down dim and then right up again. After she left, Bob and Dorothy sat in the library for an hour and watched the lights, just to see what they would do. They leveled off immediately and never varied from then on.

Bob Bradley thinks all this gives factual evidence that there is such a thing as "odic" force, and he is endeavoring to find some way to prove it scientifically. He and Philip, the inventor in the family, have been working together in an attempt to conceive a machine by which electromagnetic aspects of whatever these forces are that cause the manifestations can be measured and evaluated.

Another chandelier at Bradmar keeps busy, but in its own fashion. The immense bronze chandelier in the great hall has a habit of bobbing up and down on its long heavy chain. The first time this happened members of the family thought there was an earthquake. When they observed that nothing else was moving, they had to find some other explanation. Karl Vogel then decided someone must be in the attic fooling with it. He raced up there, shouting, "For Christ's sake, take it easy. There's just a little cotter pin holding that up!" But no one was in the attic.

That chandelier is so heavy that when Karl had it taken down so that the chain could be thoroughly gone over to ascertain its strength, it took three big men to lift it. He had a new and larger cotter pin installed in the attic, also. He never discovered any way the chandelier could be made to bounce around on its own; yet on several occasions Karl and all the others have seen it bob like a fishing cork.

Bernadette was once visiting in Denver along with her husband, Donald Thorn, who had heard about the phenomena that occurred in the house but had never seen any of it. They happened to be in the solarium on the far side on the drawing room when the call to dinner was sounded, and they had a long way to walk to the dining room. As they started across the great hall they both happened to glance up and there the huge chandelier was, bobbing up and down as hard as it could go. The delicate cut-crystal chandelier at the back of the hall was not moving at all. They shouted and everyone in the house came running to watch this peculiar performance. After a while the smell of food recaptured their interest and they returned to the dining room. Bernadette mentioned that when dinner was over and they walked back through the hall the chandelier was still vibrating and swaying after its unusual efforts.

Parris, the youngest son, told me of several occasions when he had seen the chandelier moving of its own accord. He also had a story about the baby grand piano on which he regularly practices. It is just inside the entrance to the drawing room. One night in 1968 when Parris was practicing, and his parents and Sieg were sitting in the library, the four top notes of the piano played of their own accord. Parris told me, "The four top keys on the right-hand end—the highest notes—sounded by themselves and I saw them as they indented. I am sure that I did not strike them, yet they played."

Parris, incidentally, has composed a lovely piece of music— which I think is secretly dedicated to the unusual home in which he lives. It has a minor strain of exquisite beauty running through it, yet it is not in the least melancholy.

Philip, the oldest boy, has had water hit him at odd times in the house when there was no one there to throw it and nothing was leaking. Once, when the repairs were first going on, a big blob of water struck him in the face. He went over all the walls of the room carefully, then took a stepladder and checked the ceiling, thinking there must be a leak somewhere; but everything was perfectly dry.

Pelham's most interesting personal experiences involve apports. These are objects which occasionally appear around sensitive or psychic persons that seem to have come in some inexplicable manner. They are purportedly dematerialized somewhere else and then materialized as evidence of supernormal activity. They are sometimes such insignificant objects that there seems to be no possible use for them or reason for their appearance; and yet they arrive in ways that cannot be explained normally. For instance, Dorothy was carrying her purse one day, had just looked in it for her handkerchief, and a few moments later opened it again. There were three green plastic mermaids each about two inches high, lying on her handkerchief. No one else had been near her purse, Dorothy declares. She can account for their arrival only as apports.

Pelham's apports are just as useless, but just as amazing, for they too have arrived in such unusual ways that normal explanations seem to be ruled out. His mother showed me what appeared to be an old coat-hanger that had been bent into a circle. On it was a hard, dried-up object that looked like a terra cotta-colored, ossified prune. Or as Dorothy described it, a shrunken head. The two pieces of wire which formed the circle had been factory-twisted at one spot, and obviously hand-twisted at another in order to close the circle. The dried-up object had originally been a big green, fresh, juicy apple thrust through the wire. This queer object had floated down to Pelham when he was alone out in the yard working.

In trying to analyze what happened, Pelham thought at first that someone was playing a trick on him. But no one was at home except Parris and his mother. Parris was in the solarium shooting pool and Pelham could hear the clicks as the cue hit the balls. Dorothy was upstairs dressing. Pelham had been hurrying to rake up the trash in the yard so that he could accompany her to an auction as soon as she was ready.

Dorothy told me how she became aware of Pelham's dilemma. "He came in and called me and I went to the head of the stairs. He said, 'Mom' and held up this weird thing as I looked over the banister, and 'Have you ever seen anything like this before?' I am looking at this dumb wire with its green apple on it. Then it came to me that there must be something unusual about it for him to ask this question so seriously. I said, 'Why? What is there so special about it?' He said, 'Well, I'm standing out there raking and all of a sudden I am aware that something is going past the corner of my eye floating very slowly. I looked over and there was this thing floating softly toward the ground.' "

Pelham told her, "I wondered how an apple could float that softly. I've been standing out there puzzling about it. I can't make it float. It drops with a thud when I try to do it. I thought it might have been caught up in a tree and the wind knocked it out, but there is no wind. And also, there is no tree anywhere close to where I was standing. You can see my rake still there by the hedge where I was working."

Dorothy suggested, "Perhaps it was in the hedge and you knocked it out with the rake." She told me, "We always try to find every excuse. We never accept blindly. But then we noticed that the hedge was lower than Pelham's head and the object had come past his eye. I asked, 'Could it have been caught on a window and something knocked it loose?' He said, 'Yes, except that the windows are out of the line of fall. Also, don't forget—it floated.' I went outside with him and he was right. There was nowhere from which it could have come normally."

Dorothy and Pelham are still puzzled about this thing. It seems so idiotic. "Isn't it wild?" Dorothy asked as she showed it to me. We wondered together why apports are usually such trivia. There should be no reason that a Dresden figurine could not be apported as well as plastic mermaids or apples on wire or bobby pins. Dorothy told me about the bobby pins. Pelham was lying on his bed reading one night, and then he came sauntering up to her in her room with two bobby pins that had arrived unexpectedly and for no good reason. It was a hot summer night and he had been lying on his bed in his shorts reading, with the covers pushed down to the foot of the bed. All of a sudden he heard a tiny sound, and then another, and something brushed his leg lightly. He put his hand down and there was a bobby pin beside him. He remembered having heard that first faint kerplop, and so he looked around on the sheet and there was another bobby pin.

Naturally he started trying to figure how someone could have thrown them at him. But the way his bed is located in his small room he would have seen anyone who came to his door, no matter how stealthily. For that matter, there is no carpeting on the hall in the boys' wing, and the floors creak with every footstep. No one would have been able to sneak up on him unheard. There are screens on his windows, of course.

If you think the bobby pins arrived in a silly way, wait until you hear about the angels. If there is anything these people are snobbish about, it is the way they celebrate a Dickensian Christmas at Bradmar. They always have a tree in front of the window, the full height of the twenty-one-foot great hall; and it is decorated with only the choicest ornaments they have acquired over the years. After the holidays these prizes are all carefully packed away in their own boxes in the attic.

Dr. Bradley said, "Ever since we've been married we have carefully preserved every tree decoration and get very obsessive and compulsive about properly wrapping and marking each box of ornaments to be stored in our huge attic until the next year. We are quite familiar with every item and very, very choosy about what we buy. My wife is an interior designer and like Winston Churchill has very simple tastes—she likes only the best."

So among their boxes of Christmas decorations brought down from the attic one season about four years ago were found three items that they think must have been apports because they can conceive of no other possible way they could have arrived. "One," Dorothy told me, "was a horrible little thing that I never would have bought that had three silver bells with big pink shredded tinselly-stuff all around it. It was such bad taste—I don't even know what you would do with it.

"The second object was the best of the lot, only it didn't work after the first year. It was a set of Italian lights and around each little bulb were shredded silvery things that made it glow and glisten. It was quite attractive.

"But the other was the craziest of all. It was an old cardboard box that was labeled 'Halloween lollipops.' In it were half a dozen crude pottery angels, each one wrapped in a purple or turquoise paper napkin. No two of the angels were alike, they were hand-made, but crudely, and they were dumpy-looking, not graceful at all. They had large stomachs. They really looked too funny lined up on either side of the Christmas decorations on the table." She showed them to me. There was a red-headed one and one with black hair. The others included two blondes and two with brown hair. Four wore white robes and there was one red robe and one green one.

"We could see no reason for them at all," Dorothy went on. "But then a friend of ours came in and saw them. I was remonstrating about them and going on to her about what pudgy-shaped things they were and she said, 'Why, they're pregnant!' Of course, she was right! And how appropriate for an obstetrician to have pregnant angels! So we are enjoying them now, just for the fun of them. But what a weird way for them to arrive, as apports!"

I must say that the possibility occurs to me that some maid, perhaps chastised for touching some priceless Christmas ornament, might have gotten even by secreting a bunch of junk among the decorations in the attic. The Bradleys deny the possibility. They insist no one ever has any contact with their storage area but themselves.

But even if there were some normal explanation for the arrival of the pregnant angels—what about the apple on a wire, and the plastic mermaids? No, the consensus among all these critical and observant people is that they are the recipients of some kind of unseen attention. But what, if anything, is the purpose of all these silly little things that happen at Bradmar? There are no real haunting phenomena that suggest genuine spooking—it seems more like spoofing, instead. The Bradleys do not think it is that. They have learned to see a certain significance in each peculiar event.

Dorothy keeps a record of everything that has occurred. "Every day that something happens," she told me, "I write it down in detail on a big calendar, because a week later one person has an idea about the way it was, another has a slightly different memory about it. This way, I have it down as it occurred in the first place. At the end of the year I type up the data on the calendar in duplicate. Then I send one copy to my sister in St. Louis, in case we ever have a fire or robbery. There is a vast amount of material we wouldn't want lost. We have had an average of, I've figured, six supernormal things a month happen here. Some months there will be only one or two, other months eight or nine, depending on what is about to take place."

"What do you mean, about to take place?" I asked her.

"Well," she replied, "when something very out-of-the-normal pattern happens I know a big event is coming up in our lives. We have specific warnings when something out of the ordinary is going to happen. For instance, I may hear big explosive sounds in the cabinets at night sometimes when I am sitting in the library. Then I know from experience that tomorrow is going to be one heck of a day.

"Again, for three consecutive mornings lights went on by themselves at 4:30 A.M. This preceded emotionally stressful situations for us because our children came down with severe illnesses.

"A cousin and her small baby were visiting on another occasion. A light went on during the night by the baby's bed and soon the child became so seriously ill that a series of hospitalizations and surgery followed."

"I hope the child recovered," I commented with concern.

"Oh, yes, eventually. There were no more lights misbehaving for quite some time. In fact, I guess it was a year later when the bedroom light went on again in midafternoon by itself. Within twenty-four hours Sieg's father fell in the yard, injuring himself, and we received two letters that were very disturbing.

"Before long we all grew accustomed to expect something to happen when these odd things occurred. But we also got so that when we were forewarned about something, we felt reassurance that it would turn out well. We acquired confidence that in these timely forewarnings we were being watched over by those who cared for our welfare."

Bob interjected, "I must make it clear that we do not feel our poltergeists to be purposelessly capricious. We think they are taking the means of using whatever abilities they have at their disposal to attract our attention, in order to give us messages that are meaningful."

"You do not necessarily believe that all your manifestations come from the old couple who used to live here?" I asked.

"We don't know. Certainly some of the evidence undoubtedly points to them, and especially the things that happened when we first moved in here. Whether or not others who have passed on, and are interested in us are also involved is open to conjecture. Personally, I have a feeling they are."

A few sentences from the Epilogue that Siegwalt Palleske wrote for the Bradleys' book *Psychic Phenomena* seem to me to sum up the feeling one is left with after a visit to beautiful Bradmar. Palleske wrote: "We accept on faith what scientists have discovered concerning the composition of matter. No man has ever seen an electron, but evidence points in the direction of its existence. It behooves us likewise to accept with an open mind evidence of the existence of that spirit world, to reject nothing, to reserve judgment until a large mass of data has been accumulated. But we must have patience, for investigation into that realm is slow because for some reason beyond our comprehension the phenomena coming from that world are sporadic and unpredictable, if not subject to downright whimsy."

It is the whimsical and the unpredictable nature of ghosts

that makes researching them fun and writing about them (and, I hope, reading about them) a pleasure. It is their implications—the possibility that they sometimes may really be what they sometimes seem to be, still-living entities who have survived death—that make them such a challenge.

I have said it before and I'll say it again: Whatever they are, ghosts are *real*.

Bibliography

Audubon, John James. *Birds of America*. New York: The Macmillan Company, 1937.

Barnes, Barbara. "The Governor and the Ghosts," *Sunday Bulletin Magazine*, April 24, 1966.

Bell, Charles Bailey, M.D. *The Bell Witch, a Mysterious Spirit*.

Bradley, Dorothy Bomar, and Bradley, Robert A., M.D. *Psychic Phenomena: Revelations and Experiences*. West Nyack, N.Y.: Parker Publishing Co., 1967.

Butcher, Loretta. "Dad Kept His Promise," *Fate* Magazine, March 1969.

Fisher, Judge George Purnell. *Recollections of Dover in 1824*. Wilmington, Del.: The Historical Society of Delaware.

Fodor, Nandor. *Between Two Worlds*. West Nyack, N.Y.: Parker Publishing Co., 1964.

[Fuller, Curtis and Mary M.] "The Haunted Home of William Lyon Mackenzie," *Fate* Magazine, January 1961.

Herrick, Francis Hobart. *Audubon the Naturalist* (out of print).

Ingram, M. V. *Authenticated History of the Famous Bell Witch.* Clarksville, Tenn.: 1894.

Kennedy, Lucy. *Mr. Audubon's Lucy.* New York: Crown, 1957.

LeNotre, G. *The Dauphin (Louis XVII), The Riddle of the Temple* (translated by Frederic Lees). New York: Doubleday, Page and Co., 1921.

Murphy, Robert Cushman. "John James Audubon: An Evaluation of the Man and His Work," New York: *New York Historical Society Quarterly,* October 1956.

Sabre, The. Fork Union Military Academy. Fork Union, Va.: December 15, 1965; December 18, 1968.

San Antonio *Express.* November 14, 1917.

Smith, Susy. *Haunted Houses for the Millions.* Los Angeles: Sherbourne Press, 1967.

————. *Prominent American Ghosts.* Cleveland and New York: World Publishing Company, 1967.

Tyler, Alice Jaynes. *I Who Should Command All.* New Haven, Conn.: The Gramamat Publishing Company, 1937.

About the Author

AN acknowledged expert on ghosts, and a medium herself, Susy Smith has traveled around the globe investigating emanations from the World Beyond. The fruits of her research have been successfully published as *Prominent American Ghosts, ESP for the Millions, The Enigma of Out-of-Body Travel,* and *The Mediumship of Mrs. Leonard.* Her new work, *Ghosts Around the House,* will be welcomed by readers of Ruth Montgomery, Jeane Dixon, and Edgar Cayce, and will be cheered by her own growing band of followers.